Winning Friends
at Work

Also by Nathaniel Stewart

The Effective Woman Manager

Winning Friends at Work

NATHANIEL STEWART

BALLANTINE BOOKS   **NEW YORK**

The author is grateful to the following for permission to quote
from previously published material:

John Wiley & Sons, Publishers. Material reprinted from *The Effective
Woman Manager* by Nathaniel Stewart. Copyright © 1978 by John Wiley &
Sons, Inc.

New Century Publishers. Material reprinted from *Office Politics* by Marilyn
Moats Kennedy. Copyright © 1980 by Marilyn Moats Kennedy. By permission
of New Century Publishers, Inc., Piscataway, NJ 08854

The Executive Female. Material adapted from "Bouncing Back From a
Setback," originally printed in *The Executive Female*, May–June 1980.
Copyright © 1980 by The National Association of Female Executives, 120 East
56th Street, Suite 1440, New York, NY 10022

The Wall Street Journal. Material from "Sex and Romance in the Office" by
Mortimer R. Feinberg and Aaron Levenstein, January 29, 1982. Reprinted by
permission of *The Wall Street Journal*. Copyright © 1982 by Dow Jones &
Company. All rights reserved.

Harper & Row Publishers. Specified excerpt from *When Lovers Are Friends*
by Merle Shain (J.B. Lippincott Co.). Copyright © 1978 by Merle Shain.
Reprinted by permission of Harper & Row, Publishers, Inc. In Canada,
permission is granted by the author.

Library of Congress Catalog Card Number: 84-91670
ISBN: 0-345-31960-5

Book design by Beth Tondreau
Cover design by Herbert Pretel

Manufactured in the United States of America
First Edition: May 1985
10 9 8 7 6 5 4 3 2 1

To
Charles King Angrist and Charles Ray Peck

who instilled in me, and in many others,
the sense of decency and pride
in the workplace.

Contents

Part Three
Weathering the Storms

THE STEWART SYNDROME

. . . To make it on your own, you will have
to do it with or through others.

Winning Friends
at Work

Introduction

Everything has its source, its fountainhead. This book springs from the insight that effective collaboration with peers is the key to a successful work life. Recent accounts of corporate managerial "excellence" have shown what we have already perceived as a trend: we interact more often, more actively, and more closely with our peers at work than ever before. Changes in the nature of organization, job/project demands, and team performance have made this happen, along with an increased awareness of the need for personal fulfillment on the job. Relationships with our working peers have a direct effect on the quality of the work we do and the quality of our "work lives." As an added bonus, some of these relationships at work can and do mature into friendships on a deeper and more personal level.

A frame of mind, attitudes, and certain social skills combine to build competence in relating effectively with peers and building friendships at work. Good relationships with work-friends do not just happen—they must be created and sustained. Talent for the job and the ability to get along well with people constitute the twin towers of effective performance in business, industry, and the professions. After all, we spend the larger part of a lifetime at work, and we expect to derive many types of satisfaction from it—economic, social, ego fulfilling. The central purpose of this book is to enable you to develop the interpersonal skills to create and maintain good relationships on the job. These skills will help boost your morale and the collective morale of your work group. Employees who regard their co-workers as first-rate tend to produce first-rate work.

The workplace offers an ideal setting for the cultivation of personal friendship. Many friendships made on the job thrive for years as high-quality personal relationships. As more women enter the nation's workforce, they are able, often for the first time, to form real friendships with men as work partners.

This book deals with friendships in the workplace: understanding the framework, building the friendships, weathering the crisis. We will discuss why we seek particular friendships, whom to choose and whom to avoid, how to gain from friendship and give to it, and how to cope when an office friend begins to drift away.

We will discuss many aspects of collaboration, from welcoming the new employee to brain-picking the expert peer. Competition is also a part of the reality, since co-workers often find themselves vying for promotions and challenging assignments; we face this dilemma in a chapter about handling competition with maturity and practicality. We stress both independence and interdependence, always affirming what we call the Stewart Syndrome: *To make it on your own you have to do it with or through others.* This is the essence of mutualism among peers.

The ideas and guidelines presented here spring from various sources: give-and-take seminars with employees;

direct management counseling within organizations; informal polls or surveys; case studies; and countless hours of personal dialogue and "rap sessions" with working men and women. We have talked everywhere: in the privacy of the office, on trains and airplanes, at breakfast and dinner, at leisure over a glass of wine or hurriedly over a cup of coffee, at meetings, and in many cases in the presence of an employee's superiors and peers. This book has emerged from a decade of experience gained in conferring with men and women about their workplaces—the office, plant, factory, store, warehouse, bank, laboratory, computer center, or other work site. The author's experience as consultant and lecturer in management has covered a wide range of enterprises, from a small business owned by a husband-wife team to industrial giants such as General Motors and Chase Manhattan Bank. Included, too, have been government agencies, voluntary organizations, religious institutions, health care centers, professional associations, and other organizations.

This book was undertaken with the full awareness that many different perceptions exist about the workplace. Some workers, unfortunately, think of it as a place of drudgery, a dead end. For others it is a challenging arena in which to practice a profession or craft. For the lucky—and enterprising—few, it's an exciting place where goals, responsibilities, competence, and effort mesh to yield excellent results.

We are not naive, nor are we short on memory. We know, too well, that the workplace has its gossip, broken promises, mischief, and injured egos. Hardly an organization exists without its share of cliques and the rivalry between those favored and those who have fallen out of favor. Injustice in the workplace has wounded many an employee and aborted many a promising career. Nevertheless, we heave endured all the shenanigans. We have learned to tolerate bad manners, eccentrics, the endless complaints of the discontented, rumors, and unsavory bosses. All this comes with the territory, we have learned by now. Such is the reality of the workplace. Yet we manage somehow to be resilient and to bounce back. Better still, we have learned to generate respect, and maintain friendships in the workplace.

Surveys conducted by highly regarded pollsters testify that the large majority of workers express considerable satisfaction. These decent, hard-working people view the workplace as the locale where they work seriously at their tasks and cooperate with one another to produce desirable results for the company. They do this day in and day out, through good and bad economic times. The rewards they ask for are within the bounds of reasonableness: a fair chance to show their stuff, to make good, to be retained on the payroll as they continue to perform well, to be recognized, to be accepted by colleagues. At times they seek a measure of empathy or support when things do not go well. They want the workday to go forward productively, harmoniously, and with little disruption. While the thought is seldom expressed, each worker hopes that his own ego and those of his peers will not be hurt and that no one will have his economic security endangered. In essence, it can be said that throughout the countless workplaces in the United States, people are in pursuit of happiness on the job.

So, we want to share with you our ideas about how to generate, respect, and maintain frienships in the workplace, and to help you make *your* workplace a happier, more satisfying place to be.

Part One

The Work Friendship– What's in It for Me?

Chapter 1

Why Do We Work?

With his two-year tour of duty nearing its end, Ray Haas pondered whether or not to renew his overseas assignment with Boxer Engineering and Construction Corporation. In 1982 he was hired to represent the company in Libya in its massive project to develop a modern national water supply system. Ray was attracted to the job because of the challenge of working in a foreign country and the opportunity to travel and visit in Europe and the Near East during the long vacation breaks allowed every half-year. He had performed well and was generally satisfied with the job.

However, he asked himself periodically, "What's to become of my education and training as an architect? Will it ever be utilized again? When and where?" The lure of faraway places and the excitement of travel, he reasoned, may not be enough to compensate for his first love, architecture. While on leave at a one-week conference in the company's headquarters in Key West, Ray came across a newspaper account of a proposed venture by a company to construct special senior citizen residential centers in the Carolinas and other southern states. He arranged for an interview—"just a shot in the dark," as he put it—and was impressed with the opportunity to do new and different architectural designs for these residential centers.

The pay would be well below his present salary and he would have no supervisory responsibilities such as he had at Boxer. Not much prestige, either, he thought, but what a unique opportunity to use his talents as a designer. He decided to take the new offer and informed his company that he would not be renewing his contract. A different time and a different reason for working. Many of us face this kind of decision during our work careers.

If you ask most people why they work they'll guffaw, say "Are you kidding?" and pat the old hip pocket. But that's just a superficial response, the tip of the iceberg. Why we work—and why we do what we do instead of something else—is a complicated question. We'll address ourselves to that question in this chapter. In later chapters, we'll deal with the questions about the joys and benefits of having good office relationships.

Enlightened self-interest is, at root, the answer to all these questions. It is in our best interests to do work that we enjoy and feel proud of, to get along well with our co-workers, and to find that added happiness at work—a good friend.

WHY DO WE WORK?

Each of us has at least one pressing reason for wanting to work. Most of us have more than one reason. For some, the driving force is the desire for security and comfort, while for others comfort is not enough—they want affluence, even luxury. For some the aim is accomplishment; for others accomplishment must include recognition; and for others even recognition is not sufficient: they hanker for fame and glory.

A structured life that is governed by the workday—rising, getting dressed, a quick breakfast, returning home, going out for the evening—this, too, is reason enough for some people to work: the framework of the day provides a form of psychological security that many people need.

Other reasons may be therapeutic: to overcome loneliness, to push aside the memories of a traumatic experience, or to reconstruct one's life and get a fresh start.

While the incentives are many and varied, there are a few essential reasons for working that we all have in common. Let's start with the most obvious:

- *Money and security* is a dominant theme. Work is necessary if there is to be bread on the table.
- Work is also a way of *fulfilling one's ego*, even when there's plenty of bread on the table.
- Work allows us to *prove our worth* and to gain, from boss and co-workers, a measure of recognition, respect, and sometimes admiration.
- We work, too, for *social values* in the workplace: friends, companionship, pleasure in sociability, acceptance, sharing personal experiences, dining together, the after-hours chat, support, kidding and laughter, and all that comes with the sense of belonging.
- Many of us work because we strive to *lead a more purposeful life* and, through our skills and knowledge, make a contribution to the greater good or ser-

vice of some agency or institution. Through a purposeful job we gain still more self-fulfillment and self-realization.

- Some people's value systems do not include this desire to "make the world a better place." For many a worker the *feeling of personal progress*, and being paid while achieving it, is reason enough to work.
- *Identity* is another compelling reason. Your identity is revealed by the work you do. You are identified by a title, a job description, a role, a membership, a level of earning power, a special skill. Moreover, in our culture what you produce, what function you perform, how competently you do it, and how well you are paid—the work experience—helps shape your identity. In our society *you are what you do*. Work defines self in many instances and in various ways.

There are many other reasons for work and for changing attitudes toward it:

- *To break out of the poverty cycle* is surely one such reason.
- Changing and enjoying *a new lifestyle* in one's middle years is another.
- *Desire for more affluence* often leads to the *two-paycheck marriage* with both partners engaged in full-time employment.
- *Belated use of one's education and training* has emerged as an urge for work, especially among young women who feel capable now of managing both home and a job.

Special Reasons for Special Cases

- *Women*, especially, have many new reasons for working: economic independence, use of one's education and training, a more active life, the challenge of things new and different, renewal of former skills, career opportunities and advancement, helping the family to cope with economic hard times, equality of treatment, professional prestige, self-worth and fulfillment. The good provider is no longer solely a masculine image; it is feminine as well.
- *High-school and college students* work at part-time jobs to earn enough money to keep up socially and to build an employment record as a base for landing a full-time entry-level job later.
- A *physically handicapped person* works so as to focus on his abilities, not his disabilities, as well as to sustain himself financially and break away from the isolation of staying at home. Great satisfaction is derived as he overcomes idleness and discrimination and is able to prove his capabilities.
- *The recently arrived alien* works to sustain a family in a new and sometimes hostile environment, to find new opportunity and a future more promising than what he left behind.
- One *retiree* resumes work to restore that proud feeling of being useful and productive again, while another does it simply to earn extra money.

Some of the Wrong Reasons

As there are many sound reasons, so there are also unhealthy, distorted, and sometimes preverse reasons for working. Some people equate power, domination, and control over others with "success"; the paramount reason for their presence in the workplace is to exercise control over their subordinates. Others use work as an outlet for the release of their frustrations, and find satisfaction in arousing conflict and having emotional outbursts in the workplace. It is a part of a neurotic pattern that makes them seek the company of others in which to vent violent emotions. The compulsive behavior of the workaholic is, in a way, a mask to cover inability to express energy elsewhere. Those who seek the workplace as a sanctuary distort the work environment; yet they are always there. One spots them easily.

Finding Your Own Good Reasons

In the main, work is conceived as healthful. We feel good when we are in control of our lives and our environment. In a sense, the feelings of challenge, accomplishment, satisfaction, and pleasure gained from such self-control are very important. The psychologist Abraham Maslow outlined in a clear and fascinating way the reasons why we work. His concept of motivation for work is depicted as a ladder with steps from bottom to top, representing, in rising order of importance, the needs to be fulfilled by the individual. The needs for protection, shelter, food, and other basics are at the bottom of the ladder; next come social needs, such as belonging, acceptance, and friendship; still further up the ladder are the need for self-esteem, feelings of worthiness, and recognition and respect; finally, at the top of the ladder, is the need for challenge, self-actualization, distinction, and reaching one's fullest potential.

As Freud said, "Work and love are the parents of civilization." If we are comfortable and happy with our loved ones and with our job, we are indeed among the blessed.

Work has many paths and all the paths converge into one main road, with one destination: satisfying human needs. As we travel this road from first job to retirement, and as we work and think about our work, we develop a better understanding of ourselves and other people.

We don't travel this road alone.

HOW DOES WORK MAKE LIFE BETTER?

Working and enjoying it, along with good co-workers, can greatly affect and enrich personal happiness. Surveys indicate that work ranks second only to love/marriage as the single most important element in happiness.

Job satisfaction is more important to people than income, health, education, freedom, or religion as influences on personal happiness. Sigmund Freud's perceptive observation, made nearly a century ago, still rings true today: *Arbeit und Liebshaft*—work and love—constitute the core of happiness.

The results of a four-year study on work and the economy in the United States and other countries were recently released. An abstract of the study reveals an overwhelming 75 percent of men and women stating that their current occupation is "right" for them and that there is a good match between their interests, temperament, and abilities and the kind of work they now do. About 90 percent of professionals and managers feel this way, as do two-thirds of blue-collar workers and three-quarters of women with clerical jobs. This represents their overall reaction to "job satisfaction," despite the fact that they were not always contented with how much they earn or with the job description at any given time.

These major findings virtually demolish many of the gloomy results reported a decade ago in surveys then undertaken by the Gallup organization, the U.S. Department of Health, Education, and Welfare (*Work in America* report), and other pollsters. A decade ago, a leading psychiatrist stated in a national magazine that "working people with whom I've talked made it quite clear the ways they feel cornered, trapped, lonely, pushed around at work, or confused by the sense of meaninglessness." The mood of the people in the new study is also different from the general tone of interviews in Studs Turkel's widely read book, *Working*, which emphasized job dissatisfaction at all levels in the work force. To be sure, there are still people unhappy in their jobs today, but the surveys assert clearly that they are in the minority.

We are not the first to emphasize the importance of happiness on the job. Philosophers, clergymen long experienced in pastoral psychology, sociologists, and scientists have testified to it over the years. Look back at the writings of Norman Vincent Peale, Harry Overstreet, Jean-Paul Sartre, Albert Einstein, Hans Selye, and others who have shared with us their wisdom on the meaningful life and peace of mind to be gained from work. In his classic book *The Mature Mind* (1939),* Dr. Overstreet pointed to three things as the "great essentials of happiness": something to do, someone to love, and something to hope for. Optimism, awareness of limitations, humor, and patience are the signs of happy people. The philosopher Jean-Paul

Sartre emphasized that people must "soil their hands" (work) if they are to make the maximum use of individual freedom. This, he contended, is part of the personal commitment to the meaningful life. Norman Vincent Peale recalls countless cases of people who identified productive work and career success with happiness.

Most people have to work. But working, like eating, can be a joy as well as a necessity. Often, of course, the joy and the satisfaction aren't built into the job environment; they have to be created and maintained. Joyful work, and friendships in the workplace, are aims that we will consider.

*Reissued—and still timely—in 1984.

Chapter 2

A Unique Setting for Friendship

Frank Simmons had always been a very shy man. Still unmarried at 40, he was balding, paunchy, and had a stutter. He lacked the confidence to go out and meet people, so his social life was a dud. His job as a safety inspector was boring, too, even though he was very good at it. So good, in fact, that he got a promotion and was moved to another plant in a distant suburb.

"I couldn't believe the difference," Frank said after his first week on the new job. "These people are great. They started off my first day with a flurry of glad-to-have-you-on-board phone calls, my boss took me to lunch, and two of the supervisors asked me to join them at a ball game on Friday." Within a month, Frank had several new friends, a nattier wardrobe, and a better outlook on life.

"I never even thought of the office as a place to make friends," he told us, "but that group has really made me feel at home. I joined the bowling league —that's once a week—and a colleague and I go jogging every other morning. I've lost ten pounds. And believe it or not, I get a lot more work done in the course of a day than I've ever done before."

Friendships are not all of a kind, either in the workplace or in one's private life. The workplace gives rise to many kinds of friendships, with as many degrees of intimacy. Some are merely nodding acquaintances with people whose names we have difficulty remembering. Others are relationships of a routine nature; two people meet regularly at the water cooler, perhaps, or in a monthly meeting. These are not the real subject of this book, however; we are more concerned with the friendships you choose and develop—the friendships that enhance your working life. But all friendships have their value in the scheme of things—even the most casual.

THE CASUAL AND THE CORDIAL

There are many kinds of casual, occasional friendships in the office. Some of the most common, and often the most pleasant, are described next.

Commuter friends. These are people who live in the same residential area and work for the same company. They travel together to and from the workplace by train, bus, or car pool, and their conversation usually gravitates around the company and work situations. They exchange views, return to reading the morning paper, disembark at the company building, and bid each other a good day.

Mutual interest friends are those who frequently drop by to talk about common interests outside the office—sports, hobbies, children of the same age, politics. Contact with them is usually limited to brief interludes at work—a pleasant chat, a glance at the watch, a quick exit.

Luncheon friends often have no particular bond other than the good camaraderie of eating together, but they get to know each other a little better than the commuting and dropping-by acquaintances. Sometimes they will plan a lunch date in advance, in order to discuss a particular subject or just to have some uninterrupted time together.

Conference/meeting friends are those who establish rapport through monthly or quarterly business meetings within the company. Their contact is generally limited to professional kinship and joint participation in the conference or meeting. Now and then they may follow up with a post-meeting call or visit because of the need to clarify some points or give additional information, but the conversation is rarely personal.

Travel friends go places together on business. They may represent the company at a trade association meeting, a convention, a conference with a major out-of-town client; or they may visit an outlying regional or district office of the company, do an audit, or perform some "trouble-shooting" activities. These colleagues may spend hours together socializing while they travel, work, dine, and stay at the same hotel, but upon completion of the assignment, each returns home and resumes his or her role and relationships in the workplace; the friendship goes no further.

Union friends are yet another category: they are seen as co-workers who join together and rally to defend their collective bargaining rights, job security, or a fellow employee involved in a grievance case. They band together as the need arises and disband when the event is over, but they sense some bond of friendship through their identity as members of the local union.

These kinds of work friendships are for the most part

casual, cordial, and somewhat superficial. At another level we find more lasting kinds of work friendship:

The clique. The clique may be comprised of the old-timers, the "pool" workers, new professionals, the "young Turks," the part-time employees, or others. The women's network within the company is among the more recent additions to this category; its counterpart is the old-boys' club. Many of us have observed office or plant friendships in the so-called "underside" of the formal organization.

As part of the "informal organization," the clique can at times exercise a powerful influence upon employees. It can reward the faithful, compliant members of the group and punish the noncompliant through the social freeze, through harassment, and by impeding promotion and career growth. The clique generally doesn't extend beyond the workplace, except among those in the upper management levels, where being in the right social circles adds to one's status. In smaller communities, where the dominating presence of the company influences community life as well as work life, the effects of a clique can go far beyond the job site.

"Collaborative" friends see one another frequently and share a mutual involvement in the problems and policies of the company. As peers they are entrusted with responsibility, individually and collectively. They collaborate on plans, technical projects, problem-solving, and decisions. Dealing with crises on the job, putting in many hours of overtime, and resolving interdepartmental differences keep collaborative friends in close communication. This is a very highly valued aspect of work-friendship. Good communication is at the core of sound peer relations.

The office romance is seen more and more frequently, now that our economy features a two-gender workplace. Working together during the day and courting in the evening is the pattern of the romantic friendship. Various factors make this kind of friendship vulnerable and the partners need to be sensitive to the dilemma. Moral conduct, emotionalism, protocol, influence, reward, perceptions by others, decisions, and other factors may all be involved when the relationship begins to affect work performance and on-the-job attitudes and behavior.

The "mentor" is a relatively new term when applied to work relationships. A mentor is a person within the organization, usually a male in his middle or senior years, who is available to help the younger, newer employee accelerate his or her knowledge and experience in order to attain upward mobility and career growth in the company. Mentorism is a strictly professional way for an "old pro" to help a new employee understand the corporate maze. The company sponsors this relationship, just as in earlier times, in industry, it encouraged experienced workers to guide and instruct apprentices and other newly hired personnel. Some have come to view the mentor friendship as somewhat paternalistic, since it sanctions taking a person "under the wing" and providing favored treatment. The same can be said for the "network" friendship, in which women join to assist other aspiring women. Still, mostly professional ties rather than close friendships are derived from the mentor and the network.

Finally, *the "personal" friendship* takes the spotlight as the one of most value. While the personal friendship may be generated within the workplace, it is cultivated and sustained both during and after the workday, inside and outside the office. Depth, personal involvement, sharing, trust, and confidentiality mark this kind of friendship.

The focus of this book is upon the two most significant and rewarding work friendships: the "collaborative" friendship, which includes the satisfaction of working closely with peers, and the "personal" friendship, which extends beyond the workplace. These complex relationships, as well as the more casual types of friendship, can flourish in the unique environment of the workplace.

If your experience in work relationships is similar to that of most people, you have probably encountered some people who, although diligent in their work, are aloof and unreceptive and seem to prefer to get conversations over with quickly. They would rather be unfettered than connected: you conduct your business, you are turned off, and you move on. You have also encountered people who are pleasant, accessible, helpful, chatty, and sociable. You enjoy a visit, exchange the information needed, linger a while for a talk, and depart with a hearty "See you soon." But there is no desire for anything more than this informal, chatty relationship.

On occasion, however, you come across a person with whom you have a special kind of rapport. With this person there is a strong impulse to become more than just a workday colleague. You would like to broaden this relationship to include sharing personal activities and feelings on and off the job. Thus, a friendship is cultivated which in time may grow into a larger commitment. How intimate the friendship will prove to be and how genuinely you may fill the role of confidant(e) will depend upon the trust, integrity, and depth of the friendship. This kind of relationship is a growing social option.

A MILIEU FOR MAKING FRIENDS

The workplace provides an open environment in which people who work together are likely to be attracted to one another and form friendships. The company a person works for often becomes the second most important social unit, next to the immediate family. Increasingly, we seek social as well as financial satisfactions from our jobs. From factory workers to executives, workers express the need to be with people, make social contacts, and possibly build friendships.

This hardly comes as a surprise. Many of us have observed office friendships—the clique, the peer group, the long-term service group. We have witnessed friendships made with peers, subordinates, and at times even with one's bosses. After all, we are by nature communal and seek the company and the support of others. Evidence of this abounds from the tribal life of the most primitive societies to the farm, the church, whole peoples in critical times of war and famine, in the setting of new frontiers, and in modern urban and suburban communities. The workplace is an association of craftpersons, professionals, and others who spend a major part of their working hours together. We not only perform assigned tasks, take responsibilities, and get paid; we also seek the social values and the interpersonal relations that are available in our places of work and that represent real human needs.

HOW DO WE BEGIN?

People first come together as the nature of their work calls for physical proximity: they are introduced, and they begin to share space and facilities. Soon afterward, they convene at staff or department meetings or meet in the lunchroom. Later, they come together at company events such as award ceremonies, Founder's Day celebrations, and Christmas parties. They may also meet to discuss building facilities, the World Series, new displays, who's who among the supervisors, overtime work arrangements, or other topics. They take time to preen together as the company gains in competitive posture within the industry, and they worry together when the company finds itself in trouble. These chance opportunities make it possible for a friendship to begin; they serve as ice breakers, allowing co-workers to take the first tentative steps toward friendship. But unless the follow-up is done, the infant friendship will perish.

WHERE DO WE GO FROM THERE?

The workplace friend, and the office friendship itself, is different from the friendship you cultivate in a purely social setting. First, it is nurtured by a set of common concerns: earning a living, utilizing skills and talents, building a career, and dealing with any forces which threaten these concerns. It is also easy to update; you are in constant touch with the friend as a co-worker. The friendship is marked by maturity of the two co-worker friends, both grown individuals probably no longer indulgent, impulsive, or naive. Probably the most important feature of the friendship is that your personal concerns off the job and your occupational problems on the job are intertwined, and the impact of these problems is shared. Your daughter, for example, has learned that she has been awarded a scholarship and can now attend the first two years of college tuition-free. As a divorced person and the head of the household you are overjoyed to be relieved of a great financial burden. This joy is reflected in your enthusiasm on the job and in the quality of your work performance. Your co-worker shares your joy as a friend will.

On the darker side, your friend's recurring ulcer may make it difficult for him to concentrate fully on his work, and it suffers. You share this problem, feel bad about it, and reassure him that with proper medical care and time it will pass. Friends on the job are sensitive to the interaction of personal and work lives, and take pleasure in each other's presence and sociability. Companionship makes the day go better.

WHAT MAKES THIS FRIENDSHIP SO SPECIAL?

Clearly, it is different from other friendship ties. It differs from the "convenience" friend such as a neighbor or acquaintance where the relationship is that of lending a hand, exchanging a favor, doing a chore for one another. Nor is this the "circuit" friend, the one with whom you play poker every second Friday, run into at the scheduled Thursday evening bowling tournament, or the semi-annual conference of women-in-finance executives. It's not a "milestone" friendship either. Milestone friends are a different breed, imprinted in memory forever: a college classmate, a Navy buddy, or the bridesmaid at your wedding. You remember them well because they are associated with some major event in your life, you still treasure the memory, but you seldom see them. The "growing-up" friend is like that, too—a person from your childhood, home town, or early school days with whom you now have little in common. You call now and then, visit when in town, exchange anniversary cards, but that's all. The workplace friend isn't like the "family" friend, either. He or she is not a cousin or a sister-in-law, but is someone *you* choose because that person appeals to you and shares a large part of your concerns.

The findings of a recent survey throw cold water on the glib assumption that office friendship has primarily a manipulative, utilitarian motive. In regard to workplace and friendship, people were asked whether they valued the relationship because of its "ability to help me professionally get ahead." Only 7 percent of those responding answered in the affirmative. About 93 percent evidently gave usefulness little or no thought in an evolving friendship. The survey team came to the conclusion that the connection between work and friends is far deeper and more complex than they had thought. It is *not* simply a matter of "you scratch my back and I'll scratch yours."

The workplace friendship, once it is mutually nurtured, has three distinct features:

- The recognition of each other's skills and talent in the joint effort and the rapport that comes from performing a job for the well-being of the department or the company;
- A mutual concern for each other as a person, both on

and beyond the job—a comfortable camaraderie in which personal views and experiences can be expressed and the friends can feel good about this self-expression;

• Protection of each other's individuality, reputation, and dignity by keeping things confidential and "between the two of us." The relationship deepens as more personal aspects of life arise and are shared, and both gain a better perspective and more ideas on coping with the problems. Work and comradeship are interwoven in a way that could not happen anywhere else. The office setting is unique, and makes for a unique and rewarding kind of friendship.

Chapter 3

Friends–and the
Three-Way Pact

Helen Watts chuckled as the 10 o'clock chime sounded and she asked, "Do you know where your friends are?" —but with a new twist, "Do you know *who* your friends are?" For this was her dilemma.

As a member of the hospital workers union she had been well represented, and the people in her occupational group, Dietary Services, had gained better working conditions, pay increases, and more employee benefits. In the six-year period she made a number of union friends, some of whom worked in her own hospital and some at other nearby institutions. But the meeting earlier this week had shaken her up severely. There was talk of yet another strike, picketing, and withdrawal of services if management were not to meet its demands. What, again! It seemed barely a few months ago that she had been through all this before.

Helen knew the traumatic effect of trying to determine who your "real" friends are. Among her friends she counted the day nurses, her two supervisors, the Chief Dietician, the LPN, and other professionals with whom she worked and interacted daily—in addition to her union friends. She derived much satisfaction from these co-workers. More important, there was Edna Pierce of the X-Ray unit, who was her warmest, closest friend and the one in whom she could confide and share personal problems. But Edna was not a union member; she had always been critical of the union leaders and their ways.

Helen also felt a strong loyalty to other "friends" —the hospital and the patients. The hospital had changed the course of her life in giving her the training and opportunity to build a career. Caring for patients had fulfilled one of her deepest motivations for work—to serve those in need.

Many a worker shares Helen's problem of sorting out the nature of work relationships and loyalties and making the most of priorities among people in the workplace.

WHAT IS A FRIENDSHIP?

Any relationship that is worthy of the name "friendship" has several dimensions:

- *Physical presence*. You are there when you're needed, to listen or to help.
- *Frame of mind*. You are comfortable, at ease, supportive; friendship gives you an overall feeling of satisfaction.
- *Frame of reference*. You act, you do, you collaborate, you respond to situations—as a partnership.
- *Open communications*. You are able to talk and exchange views readily and to express your feelings candidly.
- *Personal commitment*. You value the relationship and would rally to the defense of your friend against others who might impugn a person's character, injure a reputation, or damage a career.

These dimensions distinguish friendship from mere acquaintance. We have many acquaintances—a neighbor, the postman, the car mechanic, an old classmate, a jogging companion. Some may be among our "favorite people," but they do not qualify as friends.

Friends are people whom we choose to be companions. Friendships are not imposed upon us. Friendship is different from family ties or fraternity affiliations; it begins as a voluntary act and continues by choice. A survey of friendship in America disclosed that 51 percent of the respondents would, in a crisis, turn to friends first rather than to family.

Just as it is difficult to find a precise definition for ideals such as loyalty, moral courage, hope, or worship, so it is difficult to formulate a precise definition of friendship. There are special features, however, that characterize a real friendship:

- Friendship is *self-generated*. We are involved because we want to be.
- It is *unstructured*. Nothing is codified or prescribed. There is no established system, no set rules, no statement of intent or understanding.
- It *gives mutual satisfaction*. For the most part, both persons derive inner satisfaction, and sometimes great happiness, from the relationship. They enjoy each other's company, survive the many good and bad incidents, overcome disagreements and frustrations, and remain loyal to each other.
- *Communication is easy*. This is the essence of a friendship. Friends are able to talk about things as superficial as yesterday's sports results and as deep as an ardent desire to have a child. Listening, shar-

ing, expressing encouragement and support, and coping with troubles are manifestations of communication between friends.

- It *can withstand change*. A friendship can slow down or accelerate, shift emphasis from one area to another, warm up or turn cold, and be pulled by the strong emotions of either partner. In a good friendship, the partners are flexible and able to accommodate change.

These general characteristics of friendship can, with some modifications, also apply to the workplace relationship. These modifications depend largely on attitude, and on our changing views of what constitutes "proper" relationships at work.

HOW DO YOU FEEL ABOUT
OFFICE FRIENDSHIPS?

There are those who believe that work friends satisfy workplace requirements and no more. At quitting time these people want to put behind them everything connected with work—the tasks, the setting, the people. Sometimes, these people feel that it isn't "professional" to hobnob with their colleagues; they prefer a formal demeanor. They imagine—and erect—a barrier between their professional and their private lives, and make a major effort to keep the two separate.

Others hold a different view: they believe that from the considerable number of workplace associates there is the option of finding one or two (or perhaps more) with whom a more sustained bond of friendship can be developed, both during and after work hours. They see this potential because of common interests, daily contact, personal affinity, and the desire for a larger circle of friends. These people like to feel a flow between their work life and their private life, and make an effort to integrate the two. They are more concerned with breaking down boundaries than with creating them.

Many people, of course, do not fit neatly into either of those categories, but fall somewhere in between. They may maintain a somewhat formal and impersonal manner with most people at work, but will cultivate a friendship with one person there. Some people, at the other extreme, go overboard and try to be buddy-buddy with everyone, forgetting in their eagerness that friendship is selective—and special.

WHAT QUALITIES ARE IMPORTANT FOR A WORKING RELATIONSHIP?

You certainly want the work partner to be a good listener, to be helpful, to demonstrate good judgment, to be modest, to show patience and to act maturely; the same demands will in turn be made upon you. For you to fulfill the role of good work-friend, you must contribute qualities that can be clustered in five main categories:

- *Empathy*: tolerance, patience, understanding, capacity to listen;
- *Discretion*: judgment, propriety, thoughtfulness;
- *Ethical conduct*: trust, loyalty, confidentiality;
- *Organizational intelligence*: a grasp of responsibility, policies, authority, systems of work, teamwork, deci-

sion-making, and the communication network of the
company you work for; and

- *Emotional maturity*: reaction to stress, adaptability,
self-control, assurance.

You also need to be aware of the very special demands
and rewards of friendship within an office setting. You and
your colleagues do not exist in a vacuum; you are part of a
larger design, and one that shapes your attitudes toward
your work and the people who work with you.

Whatever *your* feelings on the matter are, they will
probably change and grow in the course of your working
life. In the meantime, it's good to be aware of your own
attitudes toward friendship and especially toward the demands of friendship in the workplace. Take the quiz below, and score your responses.

YOUR WORKPLACE REACTIONS PROFILE

This is a self-quiz to pinpoint your reactions to different situations in the workplace. Your answers will not be "right" or
"wrong." The questions, based on research and experience in
behavioral science and management/employee relations, ask
you to respond by checking the most acceptable, generally acceptable, or least acceptable statement/answer.

Read each series of three statements and enter an X next to
the one that reflects your viewpoint or with which you agree
most. Your workplace reaction profile, based on the scoring
key, is shown at the close of the self-quiz.

Friends—and the Three-Way Pact

SITUATIONS

1. Working, as part of my lifestyle, . . .
   a. ☐ does little to elevate my self-esteem;
   b. ☐ neither raises nor lowers my self-esteem;
   c. ☐ plays an important part in attaining higher self-esteem.

2. Stereotypes and bias exist in the workplace, as elsewhere, and . . .
   a. ☐ I feel it is my responsibility to curb them and protect my co-workers;
   b. ☐ I'll go to bat for the victimized employee, if I know the case well;
   c. ☐ there is not much I can do about it.

3. Personal problems of a worker . . .
   a. ☐ should be discussed mainly with the supervisor;
   b. ☐ should be left at home;
   c. ☐ can and should be shared with a close work-friend

4. Having congenial and cooperative peers at work is, in my judgment, . . .
   a. ☐ just one among several major factors in the job situation;
   b. ☐ quite important in deriving total satisfaction at work;
   c. ☐ of little concern.

5. People who are different from me (age, ethnic origin, religion, gender, etc.) . . .
   a. ☐ turn me off early; I seldom have contact with them;
   b. ☐ can expect me to deal with them on professional matters, but not personally or socially;
   c. ☐ have been hired by the company for their skills, experience, and other assets, and so I accept the whole person as a working peer.

6. In working with people of the opposite sex . . .
   a. ☐ it is difficult to establish a harmonious work relationship;
   b. ☐ I get on well with them, but I'm always worried about getting emotionally involved;
   c. ☐ I find it easy to work well with co-workers of the other sex.

7. As for having trust in others in the workplace, I am . . .
   a. ☐ trusting only with certain people and in certain situations;
   b. ☐ quite suspicious, for the most part;
   c. ☐ very trusting.

8. Getting to know people is important, but my view is . . .
   a. ☐ be discreet and selective—get to know some, not others;
   b. ☐ have empathy for the co-worker with a personal problem, and show it;
   c. ☐ don't intrude into another's private life; don't become emotionally involved.

9. My experience over the years with co-workers has been such that I . . .
   a. ☐ regard most of them as dull and boring;
   b. ☐ like and respect some of them, but don't take to others;
   c. ☐ tend to like and respect most of the people with whom I work.

10. Co-workers are known to ask personal favors. My reaction is . . .
    a. ☐ do it as often as needed, if the request does not violate ethics and is within your capability;
    b. ☐ it should seldom be done—only in case of genuine personal hardship;
    c. ☐ never do it.

11. We are told that loyalty to the company is foremost, but I
    believe . . .
    a. ☐ loyalty is a two-way street—if the company shows its loy-
       alty to you and the co-workers, then reciprocate;
    b. ☐ most often the company is out to exploit you, so be wary;
    c. ☐ as long as you are on the payroll, you owe loyalty to the
       company.

12. Eating alone during work hours is a personal matter, and I
    tend to do it . . .
    a. ☐ rarely; it makes me feel uncomfortable, nervous;
    b. ☐ frequently; it makes me feel independent;
    c. ☐ occasionally; it's nice to eat alone, undisturbed, at times.

13. The workplace, as I see it, is . . .
    a. ☐ not a place in which to seek or make friends;
    b. ☐ a place where work friendships are possible but quite
       unlikely;
    c. ☐ a place in which you can and should cultivate at least one
       personal friendship.

14. If I were home because of illness or injury, I would pre-
    fer . . .
    a. ☐ to get a telephone call, card, or visit from one close
       work-friend;
    b. ☐ to have several of my colleagues come by as a group to
       visit;
    c. ☐ not to be bothered by any of my co-workers.

15. What I seek most in a work friendship is someone who
    is . . .
    a. ☐ more capable and experienced than I, and from whom I
       can learn;
    b. ☐ generally agreeable and compatible;

c. ☐ a person of integrity and trust, so that shared personal matters will be kept in confidence.

16. Of the expressions below, I agree most with . . .
    a. ☐ "Good teamwork results in a 'win' for all parties—the company, the individual, and the co-workers";
    b. ☐ "It's what's in it for me that counts the most";
    c. ☐ If it's good for the company, then it's o.k. with me."

17. Unions influence relationships among workers, and I believe that . . .
    a. ☐ the union blocks one's incentives to build good relationships;
    b. ☐ a worker has multiple loyalties to company, union, co-workers, profession, etc., and they're not always easy to reconcile;
    c. ☐ the law assigns rights to the union for recognition and collective bargaining and not to co-worker relationships, and that is as it should be.

18. In regard to helping the other person on the job, I maintain that . . .
    a. ☐ we are all in it together for the good of the organization, and helping each other on the job is part of the pact;
    b. ☐ Workers are capable of carrying their own load, but there are certain situations in which they need and deserve a helping hand;
    c. ☐ each worker is on his or her own and should not expect help.

19. My reaction to sexual situations in the workplace is this . . .
    a. ☐ better screening and selection of new employees would reduce sensitive sexual relationships at work;
    b. ☐ be tolerant of the genuine office romance between two

employees, but be critical of those engaged in an illicit relationship;

c. ☐ the company should have a hands-off policy, and let those engaged in an office *amour* take the risks and suffer the consequences if the affair backfires.

20. In general, I regard the workplace as a milieu . . .
   a. ☐ in which I can practice my trade or profession and be paid fairly for my work—and that's all;
   b. ☐ in which one can and should derive various satisfactions—economic, ego, social, and professional;
   c. ☐ where self-centered persons are always trying to outdo each other by fair means or foul.

SCORING KEY—AND ANSWERS

1 point for the *least* acceptable statement/answer; *2* points for the *generally* acceptable; and, *3* points for the *most* acceptable statement/answer.

Situation	"least"	"generally"	"most"
1	a. _____	b. _____	c. _____
2	c. _____	b. _____	a. _____
3	b. _____	c. _____	a. _____
4	c. _____	a. _____	b. _____
5	a. _____	b. _____	c. _____
6	a. _____	b. _____	c. _____
7	b. _____	c. _____	a. _____
8	c. _____	a. _____	b. _____
9	a. _____	c. _____	b. _____
10	c. _____	a. _____	b. _____
11	b. _____	c. _____	a. _____
12	a. _____	b. _____	c. _____

---

13	a. ____	b. ____	c. ____		
14	c. ____	b. ____	a. ____		
15	b. ____	a. ____	c. ____		
16	b. ____	a. ____	c. ____		
17	a. ____	b. ____	c. ____		
18	c. ____	b. ____	a. ____		
19	a. ____	b. ____	c. ____		
20	c. ____	a. ____	b. ____		

Total ____ Total ____ Total ____

Grand total ____

YOUR TOTAL SCORE—AND PROFILE

If your score is under 40, you have the profile of an INDE-PENDENT;

If you scored 41–50, you have the profile of a MEDIATOR;

If you scored 51–60, you have the profile of an ACTIVATOR;
—in workplace views and reactions.

THE THREE WAY PACT

Working places us in a three-way pact among ourselves, the company, our colleagues.

What the Company Does

The *company*, as one party to the fact offers many things. Foremost, it provides a place where we can practice our craft. Lacking this, of course, most of us would go through years of training, education, or apprenticeship without ever being able to put our skills to work. It affords a place in which to use our talents, to show our stuff. Moreover, through company supervision and on-the-job experience in the workplace our skills are sharpened and we become seasoned practitioners. Many workers, especially in the technical, engineering, or scientific fields, have at their disposal the most recent and the best of instruments and equipment with which to practice their craft or profession. Some measure of independence and discretion is given so that we can perform our jobs well. The extent of this autonomy will vary from one company to another. The company maintains a payroll; we generally earn enough money to sustain our own or the family's economic needs. Through its contributions (sometimes plus our own) it provides a long-range system for retirement and annuities after a lifetime of work. On its own or by law it seeks to guard our health and safety on the job. It contributes to our social security funding and unemployment insurance; we draw upon such benefits when we are eligible to do so. Other health, insurance, savings plans, and related programs are maintained by the company in the interest of its employees.

Affiliation with the company opens up a wide range of business contacts with others from whom we can gain in knowledge and experience—customers, clients, vendors, specialists, co-workers, contractors, public officials, trade advisors, and media specialists. In many instances it affords us an opportunity for continued personal growth, advancement, and a lifetime career either in the company itself or within the industry or profession. Finally, it offers the gratifications that come with the work: the ego boost of doing a job well, being involved with problems and their solution, and exercising responsibilities. Making decisions, gaining recognition, and cultivating friendships are all still part of the good feeling that comes with company identity.

What We Do

As a second party in the three-way pact, *we* provide the company with many assets. We bring our skills, abilities, training, time, energies, ideas, a fund of experience, knowledge, and special talents. We make this bundle of assets available to the company, and we add to it our loyalty and dedication. Most of us give the company our very best in its good years and bad and share its difficulties through many a crisis. We observe the policies and rules it has made to ensure organizational efficiency, even when we question their rationale.

And What about Our Colleagues?

The third party to the arrangement is the group of *co-workers* to whom we are linked in the organization. These are the people with whom we establish a bond in the workplace. They interact with us in daily activities and decisions and make it possible to attain results within the system. Sociability and companionship are derived through this tie with co-workers, who often add to the quality of our work life as we handle assignments jointly and take pride in the results. As a base of communication the group provides a ready, informal, and easy channel through which to sound off. Group cohesiveness keeps everyone in the group informed, taps ideas, and allows co-workers to exchange favors and chores and to support each other's ideas. It enables them to ventilate emotions and feelings without the risk of insubordination and to go to bat for each other when needed, and it provides an ambience of sociability. Car-pooling, lunching together, or teaming up for the bowling tournament are extensions of this working partnership. Sometimes the social satisfaction on the job carries over into a deeper bond of friendship in private life. All this provides that sense of belonging which is so important to one's self-esteem. To "make it" involves not only being a competent performer but also being accepted by our peers in the workplace.

Putting Them All Together

Each of the parties in the three-way pact is crucial to the concept of working together. Each contributes to and influences the others. Think of three metal rings intersected and linked. This linkage represents the vital issue of interpersonal behavior in the workplace—among employees as peers, between employees and superiors, and from manager to upper executive level. The quality of these interpersonal relationships is all-important to performance, productivity, and profits. It is also important for the job satisfaction of each individual involved.

Just delete the terms "company" and "profit," and enter the words "institution" and "services" and the three-way pact can apply to nonprofit organizations as well. Educational, religious, governmental, social welfare, health, cultural, and other agencies and institutions all come within this larger orbit. This universality is drawn from both scientific management and behavioral sciences. Unless technology runs away from us and robots displace people, the three-way pact will be with us for a long time.

Chapter 4

The Rewards of a Good Peer Network

Department store selling was Ellen Beach's vocational choice from the time she graduated from high school. It had many assets: constant activity, a variety of goods, personal contact with customers, many co-workers in sales, stock, services, and other aspects of the business. She had done well as a sales clerk selling soft goods—apparel, curtains, toys, luggage, and related products.

In a semi-annual conference with the merchandising manager it was made clear that her earnings would probably always be marginal, even though her job was secure and her boss was pleased with her performance. To earn more she would have to move to hard ware sales; commissions were higher and the total compensation better for the salesperson selling such products as television sets, freezers, photographic equipment, furniture, air conditioners, etc. She was given the opportunity to make the change and did so after a brief orientation period, but it proved to be tough going. Her sales were few, the earnings were low, and she felt disillusioned and disappointed in her new role.

Her co-workers were concerned; they knew how urgently she needed the biweekly paycheck because of her large family and the recent illness and hospitalization of her husband. They arrived at the main reason for Ellen's failure: lack of confidence in selling these new products. With the approval of the department manager, Ellen's co-workers rallied to her support. They helped her master the technical language and the manuals so she could explain various features of the product to the customer. They took turns coming over to assist her when she had to handle a particularly tough customer. They encouraged her to take the in-company advanced sales training program. They commended her on her progress and when she had a good day or week in sales. And they good-naturedly kidded her about a near-miss. Their cumulative experience helped, too.

The support network of peers or co-workers enabled Ellen to move from possible failure to demonstrated success as a salesperson and to earn more money for herself and her family.

Peer relationship goes well beyond mutual support in coping with a workload or resolving a work problem. Sometimes it can spell the difference between success or failure. A recent account concerning women in supervisory positions indicated that most of the women were unable to move up the ladder unless they had the peer support of male supervisors. This limited opportunity for promotion led to negative attitudes and outlook on the part of women who lacked that support: before long they felt that the prospects of building a career were dim. Many moved on to other nonmanagerial positions. Conversely, those women who did find peer support from their male counterparts showed more competence and greater potential for success as supervisors, and ultimately found further management training opportunities for upward mobility to the levels of middle management within their own companies.

GAINS—MANY AND VARIED

Apart from productivity and career success there is the invaluable asset of high morale among workers in an office, plant, or branch where peer support is strong. This is reflected in the cohesiveness among the people. If you observe an ideal office situation where people really get along and work well together, you'll notice many things, among them:

- People "going to bat" for one another;
- Improved communications;
- Willingness to put heads together to meet an urgent deadline;
- Good-natured kidding;
- Joint efforts to help the department meet goals and objectives.

To be sure, a company's policies and practices are a dominant influence on employee morale, for better or for worse; but the satisfaction derived from day-to-day working relationships with one's peers often generates its own high morale. When company morale is low, peer friendships can often counteract the prevailing low morale induced by the organization at large.

Other important gains are derived, too. Co-workers learn from each other to work more skillfully and with fewer errors. Ideas for improved work methods evolve as they work together—ideas as to how the work can be done more safely, more economically, or more efficiently. Peer relationships also reinforce company plans, changes, and experimentation. People who work together are more patient and tolerant about giving a new idea a chance, and also find it easier to take a setback and then start over again.

THE TWOSOME

Two workers who are also friends can experience satisfaction and pride when they complement each other's talents. While one may be quite capable of dealing with the quantitative aspects of a job, such as statistics and data, the other may have more of a flair for preparing and writing the narrative reports for presentation. One person may be very sharp in diagnosing and analyzing a situation, and the other may be more perceptive in proposing alternative solutions to the problem. While one tends toward conservatism in taking action or making decisions, the other is somewhat more bold and willing to take risk. Of the twosome, one of the workers may have a view that is restricted and limited mainly to his immediate functional unit, while the other has a wider comprehension of where the department and possibly the whole company is headed. In many cases, while one worker is uncomfortable with the task of "breaking in" an employee to the job, the other is ready and even eager to show his skills as a teacher or trainer. Complementary talents in a twosome can be stimulating and energizing to the relationship.

Quite obviously, it is an asset to the company to be able to draw upon such talents over and beyond the basic skills of each individual.

HAPPINESS IS TEAMWORK

Finally, among benefits that accrue from a good peer network are the psychic gains which come to any group in an organization. These include an outlet for people's social needs such as identity, friendship, and acceptance. In turn, this sense of belonging triggers an enhancement of feelings of self-esteem and status. You are *somebody*. This is a gain to be highly prized, especially in a large organization where an employee is often inclined to regard himself as just another hired hand. Being a member of a group with a friendly support system also provides a confident feeling of being able to cope with difficult situations and with occasional boredom and fatigue. You have a sense of being supported when you want to speak up and express a viewpoint. Security, psychic as well as financial, is a very important component of group support.

Industrial psychologists and behavioral scientists agree that a group is any number of people who interact with one another regularly, who have mutual awareness of and concern for each other's needs in getting the job goals accomplished, and who perceive themselves to be a working team. A group can range in size from a partnership of two peers to a large committee. The twosome may be smaller in number than a committee, task force, or a clique, but it benefits from the same psychological gains that accrue to any group in the organization. The difference is only one of degree.

SOME HURDLES

Various polls of worker attitudes reinforce the common-sense belief that most people are concerned and tolerant and possess such characteristics as good will, loyalty, and friendliness. Why, then, do people often behave differently and poorly in the workplace? In broad terms the causes can be identified as cultural, organizational, or personal. In order to understand these problems, we will try to acknowledge some broad generalizations. First, a culture which fosters self-indulgence and immediate personal gratification above other things inevitably distorts human values. It affects values at the workplace as well as in other quarters, so that a whole generation of workers can be contaminated by self-glorification and greed. Second, some organizations are beset with intrigue; they are morally rotten. These "sick" organizations tend to bring out the worst in their employees. Third, many a worker is plagued with personal problems that impair his or her ability to work harmoniously with others. Sometimes their "self-inflicted wounds" also get in the way. Envy, unrealistic expectations, unwillingness to acknowledge personal limitations, or general distrust of others are among such wounds. In essence, such factors create a climate in which relationships among co-workers are strained and, in fact, can be bitter or hostile.

WHAT BEHAVIORAL SCIENTISTS TELL US

More is known about the workplace than we might surmise. Industrial psychologists and researchers have taken some of the mystique and ritual out of the workplace. The behavioral scientists have made their point: we bring to the workplace more than just skills and abilities; we also bring along our bundle of attitudes, beliefs, emotions, and expectations. Some of these are healthy and others are unhealthy; some are constructive and others are harmful. We are what we are as work partners largely because of these factors. They markedly affect the way we behave on the job—how we perform, produce, and interact.

For about three decades several matters have dominated the attention of the behavioral scientists and have involved countless research investigations and continual probing into elements that make a worker tick:

- *Motivation*—the motivating forces which prompt one to work and to take pride in work, and the impact of such motivation on the worker's productivity;
- *The phenomenon of groups at work*—each group's structure, norms, cohesiveness, defenses, and influences as an "informal organization" within the formal organization;
- *The satisfactions and dissatisfactions of workers*— and how these affect behavior and productivity.

Additional studies tell us much about incentives, authoritarianism, loyalties, change, supervision, leadership, communication, and the effects of automation. Recent investigations have also focused on *organizational dynamics*, innovation, and resolution of conflict. *Interpersonal relationships* have also commanded a good deal of attention, particularly the give-and-take of communication and the expression of both agreement and differences on the job. These investigations have been conducted in diverse settings: offices, manufacturing plants, warehouses, laboratories, computer centers, stores, institutions, and agencies of all kinds.

Particularly exciting is the emerging concern with *climate*—the kind of environment that characterizes the workplace. Policies, managers, and systems generate a company atmosphere or climate, and people in the company react to that climate, for better or for worse. Companies are learning to place a higher priority on their human resources and how these can best be tapped. Management makes efforts to resolve the dualism of corporate and personal values, and greater concern is shown about how the climate is affected by changing technology and a changing workforce. This is dramatically important as more women enter or re-enter the workforce, as ethnic minorities find more opportunities to do high-status work, and as older workers stay on into their seventies. A good climate will ensure equity and opportunity for all.

THE GAINS ARE YOURS

In a healthy, growing organization your work partner needs you. You need him or her. The company needs both. And both need the company. These are the basic facts of interdependence in the workplace.

Companies, agencies, institutions, or other organizations have the right to expect single and joint performance of high quality. This can be a very promising decade, indeed, for an improved caliber of teamwork.

WHERE AND HOW TO BEGIN

What attracts co-workers to become friends? If you respond, "I guess it's just chemistry," you will be partially right. In specific terms, any one or a combination of factors can spark a prospective friendship:

- Similarity in age, sex, profession, status or rank in the company;
- Background or specialization (some studies have shown that dissimilarity, rather than similarity, has often been the attractant);
- Ethnicity or religion;
- Common interest (sports, jogging, the theater);
- Personal qualities such as a sense of humor, frankness, attentiveness, or social conscience;
- The "boys" or "girls" network of the corporation;
- A common experience such as going through a similar life crisis.

Whatever the source of attraction, it is a good bet that it springs from some personal need we have—to counteract job boredom, to find a source of self-expression, to raise our level of self-esteem and feel a sense of belonging, to unleash emotions when frustrated, or to fill in the void of aloneness. You want to be accepted and to work in an atmosphere of supportiveness. Whatever the source of attraction, there follows, in time, intimate talk about private life as well as work life, outside activities together now and then, and sharing of burdens and celebrations. As mutual trust grows, private disclosure no longer seems embarrassing. The ultimate gain may be security, comradeship, self-expression, and possibly more peace of mind.

Chapter 5

Choosing an
Office Friend

A factory worker thinks back on his selection of two work-friends:

"As a welder in an aircraft company I came to the job with only my skill as a welder. Other than having attended high school, later a trade school, and subsequently serving an apprenticeship to a Master Welder, I had little educational background. My few jobs had been temporary ones.

"Tom Schure made the big difference in my life as I joined this company. Within a few weeks in the shop he and I hit it off nicely. We both enjoy comedy and we had many a hearty laugh recalling the antics of Jerry Lewis, Woody Allen, Richard Pryor, and others. While he was modest and seldom talked about himself, I gradually came to learn from other co-workers about his wide range of interests. As a merchant seaman he traveled widely, was a certified meteorologist and navigator, knew the world of nature extensively and could discuss plant and animal life with great knowledge and devotion. In addition, he had been a pharmacist's mate aboard a ship, knew real estate and home-building, and had put three children through college. He could quote from literature and the arts. While he was a welder by trade, he far surpassed his college-bred children as an educated person. And, what a gifted conversationalist!

"I must confess that I deliberately sought him out as a friend so that I could learn from him. For all his modesty, most every workday was a stimulating day for me—and an educational one.

"What a contrast with an earlier work-friend! In choosing this earlier friend in another company, I really picked a lemon. The fellow was a jovial, back-slapping optimist—to the point of boredom. He could never see the serious side of anything, right up to the day that he was laid off because of the company's alleged cost-reduction program. I don't know what attracted me to him except for the fact that it was pleasant to be around a fun guy."

Each of us can look back and reflect on our choice of a work friend—and what factors prompted the choice.

Being attracted to a person is one thing: being selective is a different matter. In choosing a workplace friend there is a good deal at stake, especially if the friendship should falter. Bear in mind that the workplace is an environment of competition, envy, gossip, and various pressures. Any distortion of the relationship with your workplace friend could affect your reputation and possibly your career. Disclosure of your personal life and feelings by a disgruntled friend can be the equivalent of betrayal in the workplace. So, move toward a friendship positively but cautiously.

WHAT TO LOOK FOR

We have seen the many and varied qualities that attract one person to the other. The "chemistry" is a surface impression for the most part. It could really work, of course, just as a hunch or intuition will occasionally prove true, but it is better not to count too much on first impressions. Let them remain impressions until such time that some of the characteristics are confirmed or negated. It is far better to go on the strength of more important ingredients that make for a good friendship.

It is folly to begin with a long list of the fifty most desirable qualities or traits. "Desirable" to whom, under what circumstances, to what degree? For example, you may not want a friend who is always humorous and jolly; nor would you want one deeply sympathetic to every feeling and incident to the point of being maudlin. Nor should you expect the saintly patience to endure every one of your tantrums or blunders. Approach selectivity not with a set of ideal traits in mind but with a cluster of the most important characteristics known to make (or break) a friendship.

THE IMPORTANT INGREDIENTS

By far the most important ingredient to look for is *trust*. Psychologists maintain that trust is central to any relationship. Without this element there is only a superficial relationship. With trust as a base you can expect mutual respect and confidentiality about personal matters shared in the intimacy of friendship. Unfortunately, trust is not a trait that can be announced or easily discerned. It is a process—the process of building, observing, testing, and then building still more. A time interval is necessarily involved—perhaps several months, a half-year, or possibly a year or more. Proceed in good faith on the basis of other factors while hopeful that the reciprocal trust is slowly evolving.

Consider *agreeableness* a key ingredient. The extent to which you feel socially at ease, in both serious talk and small talk, reveals that you find a satisfying quality in this prospective friend. It is a sign of mutual acceptance. Closely allied to this is the trait of general *optimism*. Look for this as well, and seek the friend who has a healthy, bright outlook on life. *Modesty* is another desirable quality. A modest individual neither exaggerates nor diminishes his own background and assets, but is straightforward about what he can bring to the friendship. Similarly, he will not devalue your assets or personality. Modesty counteracts superficiality and reduces the stress of undue competitiveness between friends. The modest person sees no reason to capture the spotlight at the risk of losing a friend.

Various surveys suggest that you should also seek *intellectual rapport* in a friend. Many friends enjoy exchanging views, testing out an idea or opinion, eliciting a point of view, getting some new insight into a problem, or seeing things with a different perspective. They may enjoy discussing political issues, the latest best-sellers, or preservation of our environment. It makes for a more vibrant friendship if there is such rapport, and it helps the friendship to grow. Interesting people do not want an echo; they prefer a new voice. Lacking such freshness or stimulation the friendship, for some people, will eventually become a bore and will wither.

Seek a friend who is *a good listener* as well as a good conversationalist. If there is to be a two-way exchange of ideas and viewpoints, attentive listening is a requirement.

Otherwise the friendship becomes an excuse for endless lecturing.

Before long you will have to determine whether your co-worker has *time* for a friendship. Many people are under so much pressure on the job or committed to other important activities off the job that they simply do not have the time to cultivate and develop a new friendship. Friends need time to listen, talk, confide, and be available.

If you find these ingredients in a co-worker, the chances are that you are making a good selection. These characteristics will form the core of a good relationship for mutual sharing in a friendship with someone you can feel close to, see often, and be able to count on.

Surely, there are many other traits of character, temperament, and behavior to be found in your prospective friend—for better or worse. Part of the test of good friendship is to be able to accept and make the best of these. Tolerance, good judgment, and emotional maturity will be revealed as you get to know your new friend through self-disclosure, intimate sharing, confidentiality, and critical incidents. Spare yourself the delusion of finding the "no faults" friend.

WHOM TO AVOID

Three reasons dictate the importance of knowing whom to avoid in choosing a workplace friendship:

- The risks involved in regard to your reputation and career;
- The traumatic experience of betrayal in the event

that the trust has been shattered and privileged information concerning your private life revealed;
- The test of your maturity in the workplace.

Steer clear of *the compulsive talker*. The person who is eager to talk with anyone, everywhere, cannot be counted upon to safeguard private information. Moreover, this person is often an active party to company gossip, both in receiving and spreading it. Stay away from the *"big brother"* or *"big sister."* He or she will dominate the relationship. You may also be easily manipulated by this person. Be wary of the *"friend hopper."* Superficiality marks this brand of friendship; such people flutter from one brief friendship to another. There is no genuineness here.

The malcontent is not a fitting partner either. You will be filling your hours with illusory grievances, emotionalism, and bail-out attempts. Have no part of *the bigot* as a friend; you are likely to be corrupted. Even the image of association with him will be harmful. Others in the workplace may shun you. Dogmatism and prejudice are the stuff of petty office cliques, not good and durable friendships. Be cautious before you choose a person who is the *impatient*, fast-track, intensely competitive, aggressive type. This opportunistic guy may, for reason of expediency, keep you or dump you as it befits his ambitions and plans.

Selecting an *opposite-sex* friendship, particularly with a married person, is another consideration. Pros and cons are to be assessed in making this choice, so do not make a move hastily. Your innocence may not square with the perception of your colleagues regarding your workplace intimacy.

It is advisable to avoid the individual with *excessive dependency*. Some people are unable to stand on their own. They lack emotional strength and have to lean on others for approval or reinforcement. Excessive dependency, marked by negative qualities and attitude, does not contribute at all to the reciprocity of a real friendship. Indeed, it will stifle it. There is just so much emotional support you can give to someone persistently in need of reassurance or unable to be alone.

A final word: The workplace is populated with many decent and interesting people. You should be selective, but you're sure to find a friendship here. Be guided first by your instincts, then by the test of time. Will the friendship last? And does it satisfy your needs?

As you find yourself beginning a new friendship, developing an ongoing one, or enjoying the benefits of a long-lasting and productive work association, review the qualities of that friendship from time to time and be aware of the risks as well as the benefits of close relationships within the workplace environment.

WHAT'S EXPECTED OF US— THE MUTUALITY CREED

Working together implies "heads together." Both partners have to be well-informed and to inform one another. It also assumes a joint commitment to a particular task. Since there is expectation that the result will be productive and useful, the partners have to show continuing concern for being on top of things. In pooling their talents and skills, too, each one needs to acknowledge the special expertise of the other. Mutualism is implicit in working together.

The matters on which we collaborate and work together are, after all, generally the unusual rather than the routine assignments. It is usually something on the agenda that is concerned with a plan, a change, an improvement. Or, it may involve clarification of a process or control of an operation. In some instances it may be something quite innovative. Down the pipeline comes management's message that it needs something new, different, more workable, or more marketable. Targets vary; at various times the target may be the service, product, price, space, facilities, productivity, safety, or other managerial concern. Work partners still collaborate in the sense of checking-out a point, clarifying a statistical chart, reviewing a draft, or helping out on some daily task.

A code of understanding between peers is of special value if the emphasis is placed on this kind of mutualism: You will need

- *Mutual knowledge* ("intelligence") of . . .

—what is happening

—what is likely to occur

—what decisions are pending

—what forecasts are made

—what changes are in the works

—what recent events have impact

—what new information is available

—what one has to "be in on"

—what promises have been made, by whom

Peer Presence—Teamwork and Collaboration

• *Mutual concern* for . . .
—company goals, public image
—departmental commitments and priorities

—schedules and deadlines
—problems to be resolved

• *Mutual planning* of . . .
—programs
—projects
—resource allocation
—revision of earlier plans
—presentations

—strategies
—who will work on what segments of larger plans
—how plans and sub-plans are to be integrated
—priorities

• *Mutual respect* for each other's . . .
—talents
—energies
—ideas

—time
—authority, rank
—specialization

—viewpoints
—experience

• *Mutual confidence* in each other . . .
—as a personality
—personal, intimate problems shared

—expertise
—good will

• *Mutual responsibility* for . . .
—performance
—improvements
—correction of mistakes
—risks taken
—communication

—cost incurred
—joint delegations
—decisions made through collaboration or consultation

- *Mutual contribution* to the . . .

—effectiveness of the organization
—greater potential for the future

—general morale
—solution of problems
—attainment of objectives
—general well-being of the company

- *Mutual credit and recognition* for . . .

—progress
—achievements
—innovations

—overcoming difficulties
—special delegations completed

At first glance this may appear to be a very comprehensive set of expectations. Yet companies that have developed the right climate for good peer relationships insist on these qualities. In the so-called excellent companies most of the elements in this mutuality creed have been part of management philosophy for some time. The three-way pact is quite attainable and helps create the ideal climate for productive, lasting, and satisfying friendships.

Part Two

Winning the Peer Relationship

Chapter 6

The Peer Presence – Teamwork and Collaboration

After a remarkable rendition of a Verdi opera and several curtain calls by a joyous audience for Luciano Pavarotti and Renata Scotto, an interviewer asked Pavarotti if it was true that the tenor always regards the soprano as a constant rival on the opera stage. He gave this answer, and Scotto agreed:

"No. It isn't so. We are concerned with giving *the best performance together*—for our own good as artists, for the good of the opera, and for the good of the audience."

We've stressed the importance of choosing carefully when it comes to a real friendship at work, but now we must consider a different kind of work partnership.

Often, you'll find yourself working with a colleague whom you haven't chosen as a friend. He or she is there to work with you on a project—to sit at the desk beside yours, to fill a new job description in your organization. You learn that you and this person will be working closely together for a certain length of time, or perhaps for an indefinite period, and you recognize that for better or for worse, in good times or bad, this is your partner. Here, too, is a relationship that must be nurtured and developed, but in a somewhat different way. You've been teamed with a peer, you have a job to do, and you want to enjoy working with your new partner.

To be close to and work with others is one of the primary goals in our society—in most societies, for that matter—and the workplace provides the opportunity to reach these goals. Mentors continue to assist men and women to make the grade at an accelerated pace and with fewer pitfalls. Women's networks operate not only within the industry or profession but also inside the company itself, just as the "old boys' club" has through the years. Co-workers pool their brain power and experience in new "quality circle" programs and in other methods-improvement approaches. Many successes in the Silicon Valley enterprises, and their equivalents in other parts of the nation, attribute the achievements as much to co-worker enthusiasm, ideas, and relationships as they do to venture capitalism. Indeed, the booming of small companies in the over-the-counter market testifies to the many ventures which "make it" on the thrust of sound management-worker and co-worker relationships.

WORKING AS A TEAM

A large part of your daily activity revolves around you and your work partner, who may sit at a desk near yours, in an adjacent office, just down the hallway, or in a nearby building. You may expect your boss to call on the phone at any time or you may have to go to his office for special instructions, but the ongoing lateral communication between you and your co-worker is active and continuous.

As a business becomes more modernized there is little or no place for the loner. You are inevitably teamed up with someone as a working partner. The prerogative of being a recluse is reserved for the vice-president in the executive suite.

Productive performance on the job is often based on the ability of a "twosome"—co-workers as a team of equals— to work together. One bank teller, adjacent to another, helps to clarify a transaction at the window and so expedites the flow of patrons in the waiting line. Secretaries, respectively assigned to managers in the same division, work harmoniously to spare their bosses the unnecessary burden of more paperwork or a crowded appointment calendar. Supervisor and training officers put on a joint presentation to inform new employees about the company's security regulations and practices. The chemist and her aide work together in the lab, away from others, searching for an agent to counteract a product pollutant. Two clerks work diligently to assure that the payroll will be ready on time for the December pay period, despite the pre-Christmas distractions and end-of-year workload pressures.

Other familiar scenes come to mind. Two utility repairman cautiously remove fallen wires after a severe storm, to safeguard passersby—or each other—from possible electrocution. Advertising media specialists, scanning the layouts on the table, work eagerly on the kick-off plans for the nationwide sales campaign. Airport controllers, side by side in the tower, perform a split-second alert to guide the heavy airplane traffic to the ground without mishap. They depend on teamwork as much as on the radar or the computer system.

An unwritten pact exists between people who work and perform teamed, paired. The tie is there: editor and reporter, mechanic and helper, chef and waitress, dispatcher and driver, radio commentator and studio engineer, daytime nurse and her night nurse relief, salesperson and stock clerk. In no way does the team effort diminish the competence or status of each individual worker. One does not lose independence; in fact, each can gain more visibility and credit as both move toward interdependence and use of their combined talents.

GETTING ALONG TOGETHER

You have to build upon and maintain a good productive working relationship with your partner in the job setting as you find it. Peer relationship is not optional; you can't always pick and choose your partner. The company places on its payroll a variety of people who are qualified to fill position vacancies. They come from diverse backgrounds, of different ethnic origins, and with varied personal traits. The *main* requirement is that they possess the skills and knowledge, and sometimes the experience as well, to perform the duties of the specific job—background and personality notwithstanding. This is one of the ways by which the organization is able to get tasks done, attain results, and produce goods and services. The division or allocation of work is also planned so as to draw upon the skills and energies of people assigned to a common function with same or different duties. Each major function, such as sales, engineering, production, data processing, or finance, has its "family" of allied activities and duties to be performed. You are hired and paid to execute the as-

signed duties and to fulfill the required working relationships with co-workers, staff members, subordinates,
superiors, customers or clients, and others with whom
you interact on the job. To determine how you've progressed (the periodic appraisal) both factors are taken into
account—your skills and the quality of your working relationships. It is expected that you will be a compatible and
productive team worker, both for your own good and for
the well-being of the company.

An insurance company executive recently told his managers: "Unless you get the best people available to work
for you, or develop the best people to work effectively
together as peers, you'll never be as successful as you
could be."

Your boss depends upon you and your partner, working
as a team, to help him meet his own commitments and
responsibilities as a manager. The boss cannot do his job
alone. You and your co-worker are as important to your
superior as he or she is to you, and this is precisely the
reason for insisting that the quality or caliber of peer relationships be very good.

PARTNERSHIP IN HARD TIMES

The recent economic recession put workplace peerism to
the test. Thousands of business bankruptcies and closings
and millions of unemployed workers brought havoc to the
marketplace. Dr. Harvey Brenner of Johns Hopkins Uni-
versity made national headlines in surveys which disclosed the tragic link between loss of work and
subsequent effects in terms of high blood pressure, heart
disease, depression, child abuse, family strife, and first-

time criminal acts and imprisonment. Although most people did not react in these extreme ways, they all suffered gradual estrangement or loss of friends, neighbors, and former colleagues during a painful period of unemployment. These surveys disclosed that the job-loss victim pays a very high price in guilt, diminished self-esteem, and emotional stress.

To their credit it must be said that as workers, most survived against the odds. Their success is due to more than just strong backs and determined will. It is attributed in large part, too, to the emotional stamina, reinforcement, and confidence gained through co-workers during a time of great stress. Together these beleaguered workers handled large workloads with sharply reduced staffs, put in countless hours of unpaid overtime while working together to complete a company project, redoubled their energies when illness or absenteeism compounded the already serious staff shortage in the department, went through a furlough without pay, and endured threats to their job safety and health. More significantly, they counteracted alarming rumors, saved other co-workers from loss of self-confidence or status, enabled many to cope with difficult anxiety problems at home and in the office, listened patiently and with compassion when they needed an ear, often tolerated supervisory stupidities and mismanagement, and in other ways helped preserve sanity in the workplace.

TOGETHER WE STAND . . .

This bond of co-worker concern or peer relations has also made it possible to stand up to other forces. As workers, and often despite reluctant company policies and the bigotry of some colleagues, we have in this decade made possible the peaceful integration of many blacks, Hispanics, and other minorities new to the workplace. Fighting off long-held stereotypes, workers have eased the influx of millions of women in the workforce. It is no mean feat, too, that co-workers have been able to absorb the onslaught of technology—computers, robots, word processors, microelectronic devices, and other information or production technology, all of which make labor expendable and threaten the very jobs we were trained to perform.

COLLABORATION:
THE REAL TEST OF PEER RELATIONS

Genuine collaboration can help peers reach astonishing heights of performance. By merging talents and energies toward a common goal, working partners are able to produce results more effectively, on a timely basis, and with the kind of perspective that one person alone could hardly accomplish. They are able to pool experience and expertise to probe a company problem more deeply and to see more clearly the various alternatives in solving the problem. Bridging specializations becomes increasingly more important as the business world becomes more complex. When the chips are down many employees place the peer group's interest above their own individual egos. Within the group self-generated leadership tends to achieve the kind of bend or compromise that resolves differences.

Teamwork in a business enterprise has been a byword for years, but the concern for a better *caliber* of collaboration is heightened as business becomes more complex and greater investment risks are involved. "Achieving our best performance together" is a persistent theme in companies that strive for—and attain—true excellence. Delta Airlines, Proctor & Gamble, Texas Instruments, Johnson & Johnson, and others are examples of companies that have put teamwork at the top of their list of priorities.

The concept of collaborative involvement often goes beyond the particular company and pervades an entire industry. The field of vision correction is a case in point. Here is a multibillion-dollar industry affecting the health and well-being of millions of people in countries throughout the world. The technology is dynamic, the market is large, and the controls of industry and government alike are involved to ensure consumer safety. Medical progress and technical developments in the removal of cataracts and the use of contact lenses have greatly altered the state of the art. Many people and enterprises are mobilized within the industry to make this progress possible. Ophthalmologists, suppliers, opticians, sales representatives, pharmacies, insurance companies, printers and publishers, research scientists, and others are involved in this growing industry. A visit to a typical plant leaves one quite impressed with the caliber of liaison and collaboration among those in research, production, and marketing.

The surge of computer use and information processing characterizes an effort that affects not only the business world but many nonprofit institutions as well. Teamwork may be the rallying cry, but effective one-to-one peer relationship and collaboration is the core of what makes it possible.

TAKING THE LONG VIEW

A forward-looking company is seldom content with this year's performance and balance sheet alone. It is always projecting potential expansion for the year after and then the year after that. Its directors are always developing new products and producing them rapidly and qualitatively, penetrating new markets, creating new means of financing, servicing customers in new ways, and facing up more effectively to new and different competitors. Corporate dreams, objectives, plans, decisions, projects, and delegations all eventually converge upon organizational units—people working together—for action and results. Work teams ultimately carry the burden of making it all come true.

The character of the work team is shaped by three influences:

- A mutual understanding of and concern for setting goals and attaining them at the team level within the larger orbit of company objectives;
- The general caliber of leadership in building the right climate in which the peer group can be most productive;
- The quality of interpersonal relations and collaboration and cooperativeness among co-workers.

Studies have disclosed another important element of teamwork: mutual collaboration. This is the point at which peers establish integrity and credibility as a group. Not only does good collaboration promote efficiency, innovation, and speed; it also provides a sense of personal satisfaction and well-being to the workers involved in team projects.

HOW WORKERS REACT TO COLLABORATION

A poll on collaboration among workers yields strong evidence that those who work as a team derive great satisfaction from it. Their views express this convincingly:

"We look forward to the tough, out-of-the-ordinary assignment which makes us put our heads together."

"There's jubilation when we get word that our ideas on a project have been checked out fully and they have been approved."

"We have our differences, we argue, and we get sore now and then, but not for long; no matter what the misunderstanding none of us ever gets nasty or vindictive."

"Sure we work hard, but we also have a good camaraderie and we enjoy doing it."

"Our boss tries to dodge us when he comes through here because we always collar him for a half-hour or more with a barrage of questions and ideas. Yet he enjoys coming by and taking part in the rapid-fire exchange; he has told us so more than once."

"We have come to know and work so closely that at times one of us knows what the other is about to say, and in our enthusiasm we practically finish each other's sentences."

Workers with experiences like these have evidently cultivated a healthy respect for one another and for the process of collaboration. They have developed more than just good rapport; they have also built a sound foundation of commitment that should last for some time and have come to respect each other's talents, energies, viewpoints, and contributions.

TWO HEADS ARE BETTER

Many people now view their role differently from the traditional context of being on top of things and getting the work out as responsible individuals. An interview with a woman who had recently taken on the promotion to assistant personnel officer and had to relate to the production manager on matters of employee health and safety, concluded on this note:

> I no longer worry about being the only woman to visit those work areas on the production floor. Gender means nothing when I get there. My role as a partner is mainly to collaborate with him—identify and investigate difficulties, check and review, analyze and evaluate the situation, decide and recommend. We collaborate as often as necessary and talk as candidly as possible. These past few months have been very satisfying for we have agreed on most of the findings and recommendations. In the end we always come to the main points to be served—the safety of the workers and the company's ability to comply with the health and safety laws. I find coordination and collaboration to be an important managerial skill, I seem to be good at it, and I hope they will let me stay in this post for another year or more.

This response seems to be typical of the many received from young people in management who are trying to get combined exposure to staff duties and line responsibilities.

The word collaboration implies a deliberate and willing desire to invest one's talents and energies in a joint effort to attain a goal or results. It carries understanding of joint effort, usually an intellectual effort, in which the employee agrees to an acceptable approach which blends individual with team capabilities.

IT'S THE OBVIOUS MOVE

Modern psychiatry tells us that helping is instinctive. While not as basic an instinct as love or fear, the urge to help is an automatic response to an opportunity. Individuals derive a sense of achievement and inner satisfaction when they can act positively. The better the outcome, the greater the satisfaction of having responded to the opportunity, the challenge. Conversely, the deliberate withholding of help is usually a sign of emotional illness. People who are unduly skeptical, bitter, fearful, or excessively possessive tend to be among those most unresponsive to the call for helping another.

In one way or another, all of us help manage each other's output and utilize each other's competencies. Many of the following ways of helping may seem obvious or old-hat to you, but perhaps one or more will strike a new chord or expand your awareness.

Meeting Deadlines

It is not uncommon for one co-worker to help another meet his or her deadlines. Help should be available even for the co-worker who may be dilatory or negligent. A well-placed nudge may be sufficient to do the trick in some situations; in others more drastic, repeated measures of behavioral change are needed. Even in cases where the co-worker is attentive and prompt in getting on top of things, his work on the project may be superficial or otherwise lacking in quality. Again, your help is in order, not to bail him out but to make him stretch toward more acceptable performance. A faulty product delivered on time is less desirable than a good product delivered late.

Staying Abreast of the State of the Art

Whatever your specialized field, this will help not only you but your peer as well. Explain and clarify whenever you can. Shared knowledge enables co-workers to keep in step. Things are changing so rapidly under the impact of office technology or factory automation that this is essential to the good of a partnership in the workplace. A bank, book publisher, mail order house, or police precinct is no longer the traditional place perceived by many. The state of the art is rapidly changing in these and in many other enterprises. You can be the medium for interpreting to co-workers the reasons for and the impact of these changes as well as the expectations for the future in your field. A good co-worker is often a good teacher. If the other person is a willing learner, do your part as a willing teacher.

Removing a Workplace Myth

Recently a male employee in an electronics company attacked the popular notion that women are ill-at-ease with statistics, numbers, and the quantitative sciences in general. He exposed this stereotyped notion that women "aren't good at mathematics" as a false perception, caused by a cultural bias that steers young women of school and college age away from mathematics, chemistry, and science-related courses. The increasing presence of women now in accounting, medicine, finance, pharmacy, computer science, and engineering reinforced his point as evidence that there is no such gender difference once the educational barriers are removed and opportunities are made available. There are many other myths in the workplace that are prejudicial to certain groups of employees: the older worker is called too slow a worker and a frequent absentee, the young person is viewed as an indifferent or careless worker, the alien as a union buster, the former housewife as a transient. Still other stereotypes exist: the creative person as an "egghead," the dedicated worker as a "workaholic." As a good work partner and collaborator, give a helping hand to demolish the myths and the stereotypes.

Improving Office Democracy

This is another area where your help can be important if there is to be improved collaboration. Focus on gaining better access in the workplace, particularly in regard to information. Those who have experienced the benefits of genuine peer relations can testify to the worth of office democracy. They believe in it. Office democracy implies the flow of ideas and the right to express oneself freely. It implies the obligation to listen to others and to be listened to by others. Getting an idea transmitted from one person or group to another is often as important as the idea itself. Otherwise, it remains in limbo. Access to information, especially when a co-worker is on assignment and needs certain information, can be important to the performance of his or her key responsibilities. Lack of proper information can cause frustration, embarrassment, criticism, and possibly humiliation. Your colleague depends on the cooperation of others to see that needed information reaches him clearly and on a timely basis. A poor internal communication system or a bureaucratic officer can easily block the movement of information. At times the blockage may be due to spitefulness or intrigue of an unfriendly colleague. Whatever the impediment, try your best to see that information flows freely and without undue delay.

Overcoming Uncertainty

Help should be extended, too, to the collaborative work partner who seems a bit unsure of himself. Be aware that far more timidity exists among those in the workplace than one would care to acknowledge. Timidity is usually the result of uncertainty or insecurity. Some people are uncomfortable with anything new and different. Facing new responsibilities leaves them uncertain about how to do things the right and effective way. Working with new people can cause anxiety in a person who is unsure about how to relate to others. Exposure to a new idea will often leave a timid person at sea; he is unable to grasp it fully or to accept it. Change itself is often traumatic to people not readily able to adapt to a new system, particularly when they feel a strong tie to the old one. At the root of all this is a concern about risk—the possibility of making a mistake and having to save face. Your new colleague is likely to behave with timidity on such occasions. Understand this tendency, be on the lookout for it, and be willing to allay your co-worker's feeling of uncertainty. Help him or her to overcome self-doubt and gain confidence in the ability to cope with the new and the different. Your help will pay good dividends.

Sustaining Well-Established Standards

Your help is needed to hold the line or even improve performance standards for the collaborative team. Otherwise, there is a tendency to cut corners or try to get by with less than the best effort. Many managers resort to threat and demand in order to exercise control; they manifest their toughness in voice, gesture, or memo. Tough-mindedness, however, is different from toughness. It is a state of mind generated by the work-team itself in regard to the work product. It is born out of pride and the desire to present the best possible product to the next higher level of management or to another department. Collaborators who are tough-minded have little patience with mediocrity. They show low tolerance for a project or job handled in a shoddy manner, refuse to accept a poorly presented report, and shun an incomplete or hastily prepared one. Tough-minded team members are determined to keep higher performance standards, and will question or criticize a plan that lacks depth or substance.

The spirit of the group is such that each member is inspired to stretch toward higher professional performance—for himself, for the group, and for the company. This insistence upon standards improves planning and prevents crises in operations.

An executive for a pharmaceutical company recently recalled two incidents of peer collaboration that had impressed him when he took office at a $105,000 salary some years ago. At the time, one incident seemed positive and the other, negative. First, there was a colorful bouquet of flowers on his table as an expression of welcome from the immediate staff. Second, there was a brief meeting that first morning in which his boss and several executive colleagues bemoaned the poor lab-research record of the past year. His boss concluded depressingly, "Another year like this and we'll all go down with a sinking ship—including you, Flanagan." What a baptism! For some days afterward he wasn't quite sure of the symbolism behind those fresh flowers. Finally he got the message: research, production, and marketing would have to work vigorously together to produce some new pharmaceutical product that could go commercial quite soon. No delays, no alibis. Nothing less than complete and sustained collaboration would be acceptable. The operational problems and solutions could follow. This was the essence of breaking him in on the new executive job. Fortunately for him, he was able to read the signs: team effort is paramount. He could never fly solo here. He realized that the meeting wasn't a negative after all!

BUILDING A PEER NETWORK

As organizations modernize and change, lateral communication becomes more important than ever before. Peerism or collegiality has so elevated the importance of lateral communication that in many organizations it has become the dominant vehicle for transacting business internally.

To be sure, upward communication through the chain of command and downward communication from supervisor to subordinate still exists and necessarily must. Without these there would be organizational anarchy. They provide the channels for goal-setting, reports, instructions, planning control, policy and procedure compliance, evaluation of results, and other management requisites. However, much more of the dynamics of communication occurs among people more or less at the same responsibility level. Departmental priorities, operational activities, and decisions are increasingly conceived or executed in the middle and lower ranks through decentralization of authority. As peers collaborate, they handle crises, resolve differences, revise plans, and solve problems. Decision-making is expedited as communication barriers are removed.

You find the spotlight on lateral relationships as the economy shifts from a machine-and-products orientation to an information-and-people orientation. Sometimes a twosome, a team of equals, is involved, but more often the peer network extends to a larger circle of perhaps four or five co-workers so that several specializations and viewpoints can converge upon the particular task or problem. Clear and effective lateral communication, between two people or among five or more, becomes a vital factor in collaboration. One finds it in computer centers, banking, insurance, publishing, airlines, and other enterprises. Lateral communication is also the basis for good performance in the growing volunteerism in nonprofit institutions—hospitals, universities, social service agencies, performing arts centers, and other organizations.

When you take a new job or re-evaluate your present one, consider the importance of knowing exactly who your peers are. Study the organization and find out who's who at your level, in each department. Instead of concentrating on pleasing or impressing the people at a higher level, make friends with your "equals" throughout the company. Discuss the functions of each department—how it works, what it really does, how you can relate to it—and cultivate at least one friend or confidant in each area of your workplace.

GROWING TOGETHER

A network of peers can be a huge advantage to everyone involved. As information and ideas are shared, you and your colleagues will be "up on" such important news as:

- New projects;
- Job opportunities in other departments;
- Company activities;
- Long-range company plans.

You and your peers may be at entry level or low-to-middle management jobs now, but you may well be the bosses and high executives of tomorrow. Your network of work contacts will grow as you grow.

Added to the usefulness of the peer network is the pleasure that comes from working and socializing with people at your level of achievement. You're likely to have similar interests, similar hobbies, similar problems. Collaboration and friendship on the job—and, let's hope, off the job as well, if you and your teammates turn out to be real friends—can make the "lateral network" a true boon.

SOME GUIDELINES FOR COLLABORATING

Collaboration should be viewed as a productive coexistence rather than just a tolerable liaison. Differences in viewpoint and judgment will occur, no doubt, but you cannot settle for just amity. *Results* are expected.

- Begin with mutual agreement and acceptance of the goal, the central task. Stay on this track and do not be derailed.
- Develop the right mind-set. You don't have to come on as vulnerable or submissive nor as bullish and strong. As a work partner in collaboration you don't acknowledge superiority or inferiority; you focus on parity, and demonstrate the capability to fulfill your part and watch your partner do the same.
- Brush away any bias concerning your peer's age, gender, ethnic background, or specialization. With these stereotypes removed you can proceed more constructively with the task ahead.
- Make no prejudgments as to whether your collaboration is rigid or flexible, slow or quick. Just wait and observe, and then arrive at a judgment based on work-related behavior.

A good collaborator tends to keep in mind a number of important guideline details. Here are twenty-five pointers on how to be a good team player. Pursue as many as you can and you will become more competent in the art of collaborating with your peer:

- Give honest and timely feedback to your work partner.
- Handle criticism well and do not personalize it, both in giving and in taking criticism.
- Cover for each other and keep the work moving when one is away from the desk or on leave.
- Show empathy for the other person's need, problems, pressures.
- Be on the alert in regard to schedules and deadlines—it will keep both of you out of trouble.
- Help to reduce red tape, excessive paperwork, and other burdens—in fact, bypass them if you can.
- An open door is not enough; have an open mind as well.
- Respect the values held by your work partner.
- Do your homework; the better you are prepared the smoother the collaboration.
- Try to overcome any discomfort with new ideas or approaches—chances are that their time has probably arrived and you may have to "bone up" on the new information.
- Avoid premature disclosure of plans, agreements, data, results; hold off until fully confirmed and authorized.
- Guard against rigidity; the capability to be flexible and adaptable will prove to be a very important asset.

- Anticipate occasional resistance along the way and be prepared to handle it.
- Respect company policies and rules; if you find that they need to be revised, go through proper channels to initiate change.
- Act promptly to resolve a misunderstanding or difference with your partner; don't let it fester.
- Keep the communication informal, one-on-one as much as possible; go formal on the record only as necessary.
- Develop a tolerance for errors, omissions, and flubs and handle them by focusing on corrective action, not on whom to blame.
- Give your partner encouragement and a pat on the back when deserved; interpersonal recognition between peers is a genuine and strong motivator.
- Be prepared to bend or compromise; do it in regard to techniques, methods, etc., but hold your ground on goals and standards.
- Watch for indicators of physical or mental fatigue on your own part or that of your work partner.
- Guard against unduly plugging your own specialization at the expense of others; demonstrate it but don't flaunt it.
- Exercise restraint at times; avoid taking on too much too soon.
- Set a good example in terms of self-confidence, trust, and optimism; it often rubs off on the other person.
- Draw out your partner's competencies as fully as possible so that you both stretch for the best product rather than settle for a mediocre one.
- Keep improving the chemistry of the partnership.

TWO FINAL TIPS

You and your peer will probably be expected to show a progress report from time to time. A good progress report that shows visible results will generate the enthusiasm to keep going until the next periodic report is due. Ultimately, you will present the full result of the teamwork.

Since one person may be more skillful than the other in making an oral presentation, decide on who can render the best performance and do not let ego get in the way of this choice.

Chapter 7

Confiding and Helping – Two Ways to Build a Friendship

Vera Gordon couldn't contain it anymore; her anxiety was so great that she felt she would burst unless she could release her emotions. Her son, nineteen-year-old Matt, had been informed that his driver's license had been suspended for one year and his insurance company had withdrawn the auto insurance policy, because he had incurred three violations: one for passing through a red light and two for speeding. A charge of driving while intoxicated had been dropped. The car-happy Matt threatened that if his dad or mom could not come up with the money to engage a first-rate lawyer to regain his license and insurance, he would steal a car and drive illegally.

Vera couldn't concentrate on her work, incurred more absences, and was beset by fear that her son might go through with the threat and be arrested for car theft or burglary. At lunchtime she sought out her close work-friend, Smitty, and confided the entire matter to him. Smitty tried to allay her fears, and suggested they take a walk to Building H where the company's Legal Counsel office was located. Together they related the entire story to one of the older and more experienced attorneys. He explained that they handle only company matters, of course, but listened well and made several suggestions to Vera. Through a private lawyer he recommended, Vera was able to have the case reviewed and the suspension reduced from one year to a half-year. An out-of-state insurance company was willing to issue a new insurance policy but at a very high premium rate in view of the young man's age and record of violations. The Gordon family paid dearly for it, but at least Vera now had peace of mind and could give full time and attention to her job.

Smitty came through in helping to resolve a co-worker's personal problem which had in turn produced a serious work problem. He has kept the incident entirely confidential to this day. There is a place for the confidant(e) in the workplace, especially in times of anxiety and stress.

Relating to people in the office involves many of the same attitudes, outlooks, and actions that we bring to private relationships. We bring our selves to all our contacts with people—our basic temperament, our fears and insecurities, our enthusiasms. If we are shy, we react shyly at the office. If we are gregarious, we make efforts to be friendly to everyone at work. If we are reserved—many people describe themselves as "private people"—we may hold ourselves aloof from others as a matter of principle.

What we sometimes fail to realize is that there are advantages in changing our behavior patterns. Often a different way of relating to people may work better than our habitual ones. Often, too, we are unaware of the ways in which others perceive us; we are chilly without meaning to be.

Everyone wants to do well at work. We want to enhance our own position, fit in with the company, get ahead. All too often we overlook the *personal* aspects of our working lives and have to be reminded of the importance of good relations with the other people in the workplace.

IT'S MORE THAN JUST "GETTING ALONG"

Most people are fairly good-natured, cooperative, and affable, but being amicable and reasonable isn't enough. How can we go *beyond* politeness and cooperation with our peers to build relationships—and, ultimately, friendships—that have real depth and substance. There are two major highways that lead to the friendship destination: confiding and helping.

LEARNING TO CONFIDE

Sharing confidences with a peer or co-worker is a unique activity in the workplace. No other asset of its kind is to be found in the modern company, despite the wide range of services and benefits open to employees. Where, in the course of a working day, can a worker express hurt, loss, or guilt without running the risk of being seen as insubordinate or as a weeper? Where can one express joy, pride, or elation without appearing somewhat odd or without one's enthusiasm seeming to be out of place? The opportunity to confide in a work friend offers that opportunity. Some people perceive its uniqueness and accessibility and tap it wisely. Many others are too reserved to approach it. Still others are oblivious to the opportunity or even scornful of it.

Start with the one co-worker with whom you already have a harmonious work relationship. If a bond of trust has slowly evolved, you may be ready to confide in that person or have him or her confide in you. With tested trust as the base, you can expect that two people will build mutual respect and keep in confidence those personal matters entrusted and shared in the friendship tie.

Why Confide?

The act of confiding in another has a sound psychological basis: it is a channel for emotional release. The psychiatrist Dr. David Viscott touches upon this when he refers to "getting out of emotional debt." A person becomes free of "emotional indebtedness" when his or her known and understood feelings are accepted by others.

Three reasons account for the desire to confide in another person:

- To reinforce the ego;
- To unburden worry and solicit the help of another in solving a problem;
- To share feelings about events, people, or life in general.

Emotions at Home and at Work

An unquiet mind leads to uncertain hands. A holistic theory—one that considers the total person, mind, body, and spirit—is needed when we think about the behavior of people in the workplace. The working man or woman is a unified organism, considerably more than just the sum of the parts. The interraction of forces—biological, psychological, social, economic—accounts for the way in which we behave. The workplace is the crucible of such behavior. The individual cannot compartmentalize his or her home life, social life, and work life. What happens in one sector affects the other. These incidents will help to illustrate this point:

> A distraught father, upset with the news that his son is addicted to drugs, vented his anger at the office secretary when she was unable to get the Toledo agent on the phone quickly enough. It was the first time the two had had harsh words, and morale in the office remained at a low point all week. He felt guilty, she felt hurt, neither mentioned the incident.

> A salesman lost a key account earlier in the day and on arriving home lashed out at his children. For the next two days his social life was limited to a bar stool at the local pub. Meanwhile, his wife and children felt uneasy.

> The shock of learning that he had progressive glaucoma was enough to crush the forty-year-old marketing director. Depression rendered him useless at the office for the next several weeks. Nobody understood why.

If these people had shared their bad news with their colleagues, they would have avoided misunderstandings, saved hurt feelings, and received some comfort in the bargain.

Good news at home makes a worker more spirited on the job—but those high spirits can be puzzling to others if they are not shared.

Harriet Blake learned that her daughter had passed the bar exams and could now practice law in their home state of Delaware. The elation spurred her to greater cooperation in serving her department store customers.

Ben Adelman finally found a suitable apartment, and just the right deal, after a long stretch of living in motels and temporary lodging. Now he could devote himself fully to that new system of production planning/inventory control at the factory.

Frank Fiddler talked things over with the claims adjuster once again, and this time the insurance company agreed to pay as much as 80 percent to cover the loss of his book collection in a recent fire. After weeks of being given the run-around he is now pleased with the outcome and can bring to a halt the absenteeism and the many phone calls which had eaten into his time. The foreman was soon to see Frank at his best once again in the electrical shop.

In these cases, also, the news was not shared. Even though the results were all positive, something was lost— the chance to exchange news and share someone else's experience fully.

Mind and body are integrated. Emotional transference

from home to job and from job to home is inevitable—and desirable. The psyche is vulnerable to both environments, Some people are more stoic and can contain their feelings of joy or despair, certainty or anxiety, but most of us cannot bottle up our troubles and worries without visible signs of distress. The majority of people feel better when they can express their feelings and direct them outward instead of letting them fester and erupt inward. The willing ear and the sympathetic arm of a confidant(e) in the workplace offers this outlet for emotional release.

When You Decide to Confide

For all that has been said about ventilating one's feelings, good or bad, a practical primer is needed to guide work friends in the art of confiding. These ten commandments should be helpful to you:

1. *Sort out the kind of confidences you are willing to share*. Some are work related and deal with your status and feelings as an employee. Others are home-related matters. Both are personal. For example, work-related feelings might involve:

- A concern about being moved to another floor in the building and worry that management has something negative in mind;
- Feeling miffed when not invited to a meeting, especially if one had participated in earlier meetings of this group;
- Resentment when someone else is given a coveted assignment;

- Annoyance that after a great deal of work a supervisor returned a report with a simple "o.k." and his
  initials, with no other comments.

These and other work-related matters should be expressed to one confidant(e) rather than voiced publicly.

Home-related items are more private and possibly intimate. They might include:

- Strain with the landlord;
- A misunderstanding that led to an argument be-
  tween mother and daughter;
- Concern about taking too much medication for re-
  curring headaches;
- A puzzling letter from an ex-husband;
- Lack of money to replace the old and drab living
  room furniture and carpeting.

These concerns should also be shared with a single confi-
dant(e) who can be trusted.

2. Move slowly and thoughtfully from one stage to the
next. Having tested out some lesser personal matters with
your work friend, move on to more delicate or sensitive
topics you might be willing to share. Later, as the two of
you continue to be comfortable as well as trusting, move
on to more intimate matters.

3. As you confide, make it a point to find a place where
you are assured some measure of privacy. Avoid being
overheard by others in the vicinity of your desk, lunch
table in the cafeteria, elevator, restroom, lobby, or other
open facility.

4. Expect that the communication is likely to be some-what unlike the leisurely conversations you can have in the home of an old friend. At work the sharing of information may have to be very brief despite the intensity of feeling or depth of the problem. Often more "body language" is used—movements of the head, eyes, hands, and shoulders. Gestures, manners, and facial expressions convey emotions and thoughts in nonverbal communication. A nod of the head can signal a pledge of trust. Learn this "emotional shorthand" and practice it when time is limited.

5. Be aware that quite often the exchange will not be concluded. For various reasons it may be necessary to call a halt to the discussion and continue with it another time. If your work friend is clearly agitated, don't delay the follow-up. Try to meet after hours to continue the discussion. Interruption of a serious conversation can be very distressing.

6. Be a *good* listener, not merely a willing one. The skillful listener is one who listens and deliberates at the same time, "taking in" words, ideas, and emotions, and watching for gestures and then restructuring them into a meaningful whole. A good confidant(e) does evaluational listening.

7. Be prepared for some conversations which will be replete with resentment and anger. Be able to handle anger and to calm your work friend. Much has been written about how to deal with anger effectively.

8. Be cautious about giving advice which should more appropriately come from a professional. Your work friend may pose a problem that calls for the expertise of an attorney, physician, accountant, broker, social worker, insurance official, building inspector, or other qualified person. In such cases you fulfill your role of confidant(e) well, after listening carefully, by referral to a competent source for advice.

9. Shy away from writing any confidential memos or letters. Good trusted friends can communicate well enough orally. It is prudent for several reasons to avoid writing:

- The written word can be misinterpreted;
- The letter might be misrouted and fall into the wrong hands;
- If the friendship should break up in the future it is comforting to know that residual material cannot be misused.

10. An image has persisted that two people can accomplish an intimate sharing of confidence only over drinks. It is time to shatter the stereotype of the drinking partners unburdening their woes as the bartender continues to pour the next round. Neither alcohol nor bar stool are necessary or helpful for confiding. Try to stay away from this kind of setting unless it's the only place available or the occasion really seems to call for a drink.

No Slip-up, No Blunder

More important than any single rule or commandment is the overall need to respect confidentiality. Integrity and trust are a must. Keeping secrets is the Golden Rule of sharing confidences.

Lapses do occur, unfortunately, and sometimes confidences are breached. This hurts the friend and the friendship. Guard against such lapses and be aware of the possible causes of an inadvertent breach. *Loose talk* is the main offender. *Indiscretion* ranks close. *Curiosity*—just plain nosiness—is often a cause of leakage. *Boredom* and the need for a bit of drama could lead to disclosure of personal information.

Another danger lies in the underground traffic in information in the company. Some workplaces are staid and proper, and personal information is easily kept private. In many a workplace, however, there appears to be permanent open season on gossip, nosiness, and intrusion into the private lives of others. People thrive on it and the air is filled each morning with the latest dope about who's been doing what to whom. People are naturally gregarious and sometimes that gregariousness leads to thoughtless mischief. Unfortunately, it's a difficult task to curb the tongues of people who disrupt morale or bring hurt to others. We have an ethical obligation to respect our own confidences and other people's. It is a matter of integrity.

Understand Some of the Perils

Sensitive personal topics shared in confidence cover a wide range of both work-related and home-related items.

Some are "safe" and others are perilous. These are among the most critical areas—the ones where the confidant(e) has to guard most carefully against slip-ups or blunders.

Moonlighting. If the work friend is holding down another job to earn more money, keep it quiet. Discuss it with him only if you sense that it is affecting the performance of his primary job (i.e., energy, concentration, attendance, quality, etc.). Warn him if word is getting around that others have noted that the performance has slackened.

Gambling. Gambling, particularly betting on the horses or at the casino tables, often becomes a conversation piece. Suggest to your friend that he or she place bets through an outside public phone and restrain the elation at winning or the gloom when he loses. Co-workers and superiors tend to relate the gambling habit to unreliability and indebtedness. It also diverts attention from the job. Gambling is, after all, an addiction.

Affirmative Action. Affirmative action has its defenders and its detractors. The question of quotas remains a debatable issue. You are entitled to your convictions as you develop friendship with a minority member. Remember that under the law he or she has the right to equal opportunity but not necessarily to preference. The issue can become sensitive when it relates to a promotion, transfer, layoff, or other personnel action. If your friend contemplates a grievance action, advise that it be pursued on the merits of the case. Fulfill your confidentiality role by showing empathy, explaining as best you can, and preventing disclosure of your friend's intentions. The employee deserves his or her fair chance. Whatever the outcome, you and other co-workers should prudently accept it after higher management has made its judgment.

Mobility. Within the range of options in a democratic society, anyone can seek a change to advance his or her career. If your friend plans to look around for another job, you may want to discuss the pros and cons of this action. Guard this private information most carefully, for inadvertent disclosure could jeopardize your friend's current job. He may already have strained the relationship with his superior who somehow has wind of it, but that is a matter to be resolved between them. Stay discreetly clear of it.

Sexuality. This is a very private matter. The issue of "straight" or "gay" or the matter of fidelity or infidelity is a moral judgment. As a peer in the workplace it is not appropriate for you to make moral judgments for or about others. The desire to confide about sexual matters that produce anxiety and stress is understandable. Good friends discuss these matters often and at some length. Maturity and confidentiality, good listening and good dialogue may often be all that is needed by your work friend.

Ethics. Friendship and confidence can be abused. Don't yield to unethical conduct under the large umbrella of "loyalty." Shun the proposal if your friend asks your support and plans to falsify a record, commit an irregularity in regard to company funds, tamper with the computer, or testify falsely against another. If you wish to cover up for him or reinforce an alibi, you may accede, but draw the line when it borders on violation of ethics; do not be a participant.

Alcohol or Drugs. Addiction to alcohol or drugs is an increasingly vexing problem about which co-workers seek to share their worries. Encourage positive action to break away from the habit. Help your friend to seek out the best referral to sources of professional expertise. The company itself often knows of such referrals as part of its employee rehabilitation program, though many workers are wary of the company's ability to assure privacy of information. If your friend's work performance is visibly affected because of the habitual use of alcohol or drugs, or if all your advice and supportive efforts seem to be in vain, you may have to terminate the personal friendship with your peer. It seems unfair, perhaps, but at some point your association with him could injure your own reputation in the workplace. Give it sympathetic and serious thought.

Performance Appraisal. Performance appraisal, again, is one of those subjects candidly discussed between work friends, but ultimately becomes a matter between your peer and his superior. Since salary increases, prospective promotions, and careers are often affected by a performance appraisal, feelings run high if the appraisal is not entirely favorable. If your friend can use good advice on how to handle the follow-up oral phase of the evaluation, proffer the advice. Or, if your peer feels hurt over what he regards to be an unjust appraisal or rating and needs to know the formal machinery by which to prepare a grievance and best handle the case, then surely provide him with the information. Stop short, however, of interceding or trying to influence the superior to change the rating. Your well-intentioned action in support of your friend may backfire and make things all the more complicated.

Other Confidential Matters. Varied bits of personal information become known in the course of the work friendship. Among these are military service record, test scores, indebtedness, medical history, a previous run-in with the law, an earlier marriage, an adoption, and other information. Keep it all strictly private and confidential.

Distance Can Be Deceptive

One observation regarding the sensitivity of colleagues' behavior while traveling for the company: You may be some 400 miles away from the company's quarters, and still be on company business. While the company will generally not monitor your off-hours conduct, be aware that upon your return the discussion of some incident could be misinterpreted. These days men and women often travel together to represent the company. Their many hours spent together can raise sensitive questions among the curious and the prudish. They can also give rise to an unexpected—and perhaps unsought or inappropriate—revelation of confidences. If a colleague shares with you personal happenings that go beyond the bounds of accepted sociability, keep the information private. Too much is at stake that can affect the reputations and careers of both of you.

You Can Turn a Deaf Ear

Don't be afraid to refuse to hear confidences or to make clear to your colleague that you don't wish to share intimate information. Try to allay his or her anxiety and worry, of course, but don't allow yourself to be drawn in more deeply than you wish. Sometimes diverting the conversation to a lighter or more general topic will actually help the person; perhaps his or her problem is even illusory. Recall that gem expressed by the noted publisher, Gardner Cowles, on his 80th birthday:

> Once I was young. Now, I'm old. I've had many troubles—most of them never happened.

LEARNING TO HELP

Doing things together underlines friendship—doing things together socially or doing work together at the office. This is desirable, of course, but far more significant is doing things *for* each other, professionally and personally.

Question: How can you help your friend to become a better work-person in skills, work habits, and general relationships?

Answer: Offer him the benefit of your knowledge and skill in attaining better performance; and do it tactfully. He will probably take you up on it.

Question: How?

Answers: If your duties are more or less side-by-side with those of the co-worker, he or she may seek your advice on how to reduce errors or waste in performing certain duties. Some people teach each other the tricks of doing certain tasks more easily and quickly. Show your friend what *you* have learned, and see what he or she has to teach you in return.

Be concerned if you observe signs of chronic absenteeism or excessive lateness on the part of your co-worker. Let him know—discreetly—when you feel that he may be on the carpet for disciplinary action because of abuse of employee attendance.

A good friend levels with the co-worker to avert trouble with his superiors. Failing to meet a deadline, for example, is one of those trouble spots. Help him allocate his time and priorities better and to meet deadlines. It will not only help him but will serve the department as well.

Help your friend learn how to take criticism on the job. Many a co-worker has his ego injured when the boss or other official criticizes his performance. Help your friend to understand that constructive criticism is a path to improvement. If you think the criticism is unwarranted or unduly harsh, don't hesitate to say so, but if it is valid and in the best interests of improved work performance, then urge him to see the criticism as constructive.

Stress the point that feedback of one's strong and weak points can enable him to improve his work. Recognize that you are dealing with a person whose ego has been deflated, and try to allay his hurt and restore his self-confidence at the same time that you advise him about taking criticism constructively.

If your friend is quick-tempered and tends to be explosive, help him or her to learn the importance of self-control. Point out the lack of maturity and the poor image conveyed when he erupts in this way. Repeated displays of anger become disruptive to the workplace. To the extent that you can, teach him the importance of restraint and self-control.

Good friends represent each other in a favorable light to others. Put in a good word whenever it is appropriate and point up some original work or special project for which he should be credited. If his visibility is deserved, then it warrants recognition. As the opportunity arises at a luncheon, a meeting, a chance conversation, try to bring his good work into the open so that he will get credit for it. The supervisor—who should be the one to do it—is often negligent or unwilling to acknowledge a good job done. Too many cases of supervisory inaction or "credit snatching" deprive the worker of his due. A word of caution: do not engage in salesmanship to boost your co-worker; this will not only be foolish but would also backfire. Just get in a good word in his behalf when it is timely and appropriate.

Much has already been said about helping your co-worker friend when he is troubled. *Every now and then a disturbing event is apt to be magnified into a crisis.* Do what you can to put the problem in its proper perspective so that he can see it more clearly. He will be better able to cope with it when it no longer seems overwhelming. Listen well, show empathy, suggest several options as courses of action to deal with a problem of this kind, and keep it confidential. Bear in mind that sharing problems and feelings is vital to a good friendship.

Help the woman co-worker who is concerned about child care while she is at work. A recent survey of working women disclosed that 70 percent of women (and as many as 50 percent of men) express the view that working women will never be able to do their best on the job unless they feel that child-care facilities are adequate to assure the safety of their children. As a co-worker, be mindful of her anxiety on the job and the stress she endures when that element of safety is not assured. If you or someone else in the company knows of a reliable source of child care, and one within her economic means, inform her of a source she might have overlooked. Bear with her if the company gives her a flexible work schedule adjusted to her particular needs. Good performance is more important than ritualized hours of work, and she warrants your support.

You Can't Play God

The ways to help are many. Remember, too, that they are reciprocal. Your co-worker friend will find the opportunity to help *you* when needed just as you have helped him.

A good friend, whether a work friend or a personal friend, will help to the extent that is possible, but remember that there are areas where it is *not* possible. You cannot alter your co-worker's traits, temperament, personality, instincts, or other internal forces that govern behavior. You cannot shake up or restructure his genes. Don't even try. You can, however, influence his outlook and assist him in behaving more responsibly in the workplace. Perhaps you can help a co-worker to be more mature. You can even spotlight an obvious character trait that might harm his image in the workplace. He may, on his own, then wish to take thoughtful and corrective action. But abandon any notion of changing his basic character and temperament.

As you try to help, be aware that moralizing, theatrics, or indulgence are not needed. Just candor, good will, constructive deeds, kept promises, and moral support—these are the essentials. A good friend willing to help is truly a godsend!

Chapter 8

Breaking In the New Person

Anita Puntes asserts to this day that she could never have adjusted to her new job without the prodding and support of her co-workers. She landed her first job at Crescent Insurance only a few months after arriving from Puerto Rico, and her English was limited; she'd had instruction in high school and had "picked up" more among friends in the community, but her new job here required that she speak English clearly. The interviewers were impressed with her many good qualities and prior experience in the insurance business, but were concerned about her language problem, since much of her work involved talking on the phone or with visitors in the firm's reception area. Her co-workers, concerned that impatient or intolerant clients might view Anita in terms of a Hispanic female stereotype, encouraged her to enroll in a conversational English course at the local evening adult education center; they would do the rest to reinforce her learning. At every opportunity they prompted her to put her new vocabulary to use, sharpen her pronunciation, slow down the pace of her speech, and otherwise improve her oral English. One of her co-workers arranged to borrow an office cassette player and showed Anita how to record her voice in a simulated telephone conversation, have it replayed, analyze the weak spots, and then proceed with self-improvement through practice and drill. She was able to accelerate her learning well beyond expectation.

Anita has become fluent in English, gained two promotions of the basis of superior performance, and is currently an instructor of recently hired claims adjustment personnel in the company. She attributes her success in large part to the help and support of her co-workers in her first weeks at Crescent Insurance.

First impressions have a lasting effect. From the first day the new person reports on the job, he begins to form positive or negative opinions about the new workplace and the people he finds there. The roots of good will, rapport, and mutualism are laid down in the early days of a new job. The new person can make a quick and successful adjustment only when the peers provide a supportive climate.

Impressions, like actions, have consequences. To this day you probably can still recall your first days on a new job. The memory is probably one of special pleasure or bitterness; very seldom is it one of neutrality. You remember who showed you around, the first sight of your office or shop quarters, who did or didn't say "Hello, and welcome," the smile or frown of the woman at the adjoining table, the isolation of having lunch alone, scrambling for an uncertain parking place on the grounds. Here is a selection of first impressions recalled by others, at the onset of a peer relationship.

The going-away party for Dick Blum, who was about to take on a new job as regional officer in Chicago, was a bit

different from other parties. After the fun and the fes-
tivities a group of Dick's loyal colleagues sat around to
share the nostalgia of working with him over the years.
Roger Osborne recalled his first weeks on the job, in
these words:

> Right at the start I pulled some boners in approving
> two loans. They should not have been made. Poor
> judgment on my part, and yet my superior let them
> go through for some reason. I could have been
> canned. Remember, in those days if a bank em-
> ployee showed poor judgment in handling a loan re-
> quest the consequence was far more than just sharp
> criticism from the branch manager. You faced the
> prospect of having blown a professional career in
> banking. Very little chance of ever getting a favor-
> able referral to your next employer. Dick saved me.
> He didn't have to, mind you, but he did. He took
> me to lunch, grilled me about the errors, analyzed
> what I should have asked and investigated more
> thoroughly, and suggested better techniques for han-
> dling such requests in the future. He encouraged
> this lunch-and-review so that we would do it once a
> week. It was the most intensive and beneficial on-
> the-job training I had ever had. Within a month or
> so I became much more analytical and professional
> in handling my job. Dick proved to be a fine co-
> worker, a tutor, and a friend.

Hal Colby tells his story this way:

> I was appointed assistant manager for advertising
> and made the move from New England to the mid-
> Atlantic area. Almost immediately I had to contend

with a clique of three advertising specialists who were quite resentful of my presence. It seems that I was hired from the outside when it had long been assumed that any vacancy in this department would be filled from within. A buddy of these three fellows was passed over when I was hired for the position. It seems that they had gone to bat for him but to no avail; top management had decided that someone with stronger credentials was needed. Well, when word circulated that the "outsider" was to arrive, hostile feelings were expressed and it was feared that this clique would sabotage me.

It was touch-and-go those first several weeks on the job. These three specialists, who worked for me now, would quarrel with me about anything and everything—assignments, projects, copy, revisions, budget, etc. The days were arduous, believe me, and I had to exercise the utmost restraint to avoid blowing up.

But soon other managers in the marketing division came by to greet me, wished me well, and indicated their good will to help where they could. More important, however, they reassured me confidentially that the resentful few would pose no more than a surface threat. In due course the clique backed off and the tension eased, as the managers predicted it would.

The advice and support of my fellow managers deterred me from taking rash action that would have alienated others in addition to the clique, action that would have backfired badly. I credit my peers for having given me both support and sound advice when I needed it most.

Most people view the new employee as neither a threat nor a blessing. It is a wait-and-watch situation. They are aware that a harmonious relationship in the workplace is the product of several ingredients—the willingness to carry one's full share of the workload, the ability to perform with competence, the individual's personality or temperament and manner of handling himself, and the ease of communicating with that person. In most instances feelings of empathy and rapport among workers evolve slowly but genuinely. By and large you get what you deserve.

Imagine yourself starting a new job in a company where a climate of peer support is lacking. Life can be hard for anyone who is new on the job, but a lack of encouragement can make it much harder. Adjustment is far more difficult and the transition to the new job becomes troublesome. Various firms report that over half of their voluntary quits occur within the first months despite the fact that the people were generally screened and found to be qualified. A study of more than 400 operators at Texas Instruments revealed that the first days and weeks on the job were anxious and disturbing ones.

HOW CAN THE COMPANY HELP?

Traditionally, we have regarded two parties as essential to the induction of the new hire: Personnel and the worker's supervisor.

First, the Personnel staff is expected to provide orientation to such matters as benefits, leave, holidays, security, time records, parking, affirmative action channels, health facilities, the grievance procedure, and other information.

A good personnel officer will see that every effort is made to expedite things for the new employee. Having a new employee "chasing around" after information is frustrating and wasteful. Either a staff member of the Personnel Department, a secretarial assistant, or someone designated by the supervisor should inform him about practical matters such as completion of the proper forms, the copier facilities, personal telephone calls or visitors, equipment and supplies, car pools available, services, mail and messenger procedures, meetings, employee clubs, and other related information. It is good to keep him informed, too, of the external community—its special services to families, health facilities, cultural events, religious institutions, schools for continuing education, and other community-related information. All this is part of the welcome climate toward a healthy relationship among co-workers. Yet, he will still be expected to fend for himself and to make his own adjustment to the new setting.

Second, the new employee's boss or supervisor is expected to provide additional orientation to inform him about his duties, supply procedures, on-the-job safety, call-in in case of absence, performance appraisal, hours of work, emergency services, overtime work, uniforms, and other worksite information. The new employee learns about the probation period in which he will be observed and rated on performance, attitudes, compliance with company rules, and other factors. But all this is just information; it falls far short of the real adaptation to the workplace that takes place over the ensuing several weeks or months. Here, the key element is peerism and relationships with co-workers.

HOW CAN PEERS HELP?

First by being aware of the number of things that are worrisome to the newcomer and understanding the psychology of the situation.

Insecurity, tension, and general uneasiness as one faces the new work environment often cause behavior that is perceived by associates as lack of self-confidence. If you look awkward, people believe you *are* awkward.

There is always an element of fear about a new job, especially if it involves great complexity or if the state of the art is changing rapidly. The greater the complexity of the job, the greater the risk and pressure.

Sometimes a new person's expectations about the job are great but once on the job there is a letdown. He will rebel inwardly at being lured to the new job, which he may perceive as no better than his old one.

By far the most severe difficulties experienced by the newcomer are what we call "self-inflicted wounds." Rigidity, inability to take criticism and being unreceptive to new or better ways of doing the job are among the pronounced "wounds." A new employee becomes a problem to his peers and boss as well as to himself when he retreats to the classical defense, "We always did it this way on my old job and I am used to doing it that way." Being habituated to certain ways with a former employer is one thing; measuring up to productivity with the new employer is quite another. There's bound to be a clash unless he adapts to the new environment and different methods. If he remains stubborn about it, friendly co-workers can offer a hand in enabling him to understand and work his way out of the dilemma.

A very real problem arises when a new employee fails to understand productivity standards. Some new employees don't grasp the essentials of the system and others are skeptical of how it is tied to compensation rates or eligibility for merit pay increase. Moreover, they often receive one explanation on productivity from the supervisor and another from the older employees who have been around for some time and who are usually opposed to the measuring instruments of the productivity system. Peers can be very helpful in clarifying what the productivity standards are all about and how one can meet them regularly.

Special problems are encountered by the physically handicapped who want to focus on their abilities rather than disabilities, the long-time unemployed who have lost much of their self-esteem because of idleness and must be wary of being truly productive once again, and by women re-entering the workforce after an absence of some years. In each case the restoration of self-confidence is very important. The ability to cope with workplace problems and to "make it" will depend in considerable measure on the supportive attitude of co-workers.

All new employees, and particularly those with special problems, need proper introduction to the new job so that they can become fully productive as early as possible. People value self-sufficiency but also need peer support. Sensitivity, awareness, and a friendly, open demeanor are the best gifts you can offer to your new colleague.

HOW CAN THE NEW COLLEAGUE
HELP HIMSELF?

You have been around long enough to know that new people come to your workplace in all shapes, sizes, and temperaments. Some are bright and catch on quickly; others are quite slow. Some are excessively social, others only moderately so, and still others would prefer to be loners. Some are technically competent and self-reliant, others are only marginal yet try to cover up their inadequacy. Co-workers quickly size up any flaws in the new person. Often the new employee is not aware of the first impression he or she is making, and unwittingly comes across as slower, less friendly, or less enthusiastic than he really is. The new employee, too, must be aware of typical workplace problems from the onset and, through understanding, avoid common mistakes.

The new employee is often reluctant to ask questions or seek an explanation to clarify a matter. The reluctance understandably grows out of the fear of appearing to be stupid or of acknowledging a limitation. The awareness of being on probation exacerbates these worries. A new employee should try to remember that people like to be helpful and that learning the ropes is a process, not something that "just happens": the learning process never ends, and how and from whom we learn is probably not as important as what and when we learn it.

The new employee who is lucky has supportive co-workers who will urge him out of his shell and encourage him to seek their advice when needed. The caliber of peer presence can influence the situation for better or worse.

By being open, friendly, enthusiastic, and eager to

learn, and by carefully putting his best talents forward, a new employee can encourage his colleagues to befriend him.

BE AWARE OF THE WARY

Unfortunately, co-workers do not always come forward at first, but wait until the new person has "proven himself" in some way. Stereotyping, rumors, distorted communication, withheld information, deliberate delays, exclusion from the ordinary social amenities, and other tactics are all too frequent among workers who are reluctant to help a new person. Giving the newcomer "the silent treatment" is among the most hurtful tactics. Union members, for example, are likely to make life uncomfortable for the uncommitted. Yes, malice does exist in the workplace to a degree, and the new employee would do well to be aware of it and guard against it.

Many co-workers do not put out the welcome mat for the newcomer. An unhappy man may be too preoccupied even to notice the new person. Often an older employee will view the younger new hire as a threat and will be leery of assisting him in any way. The individual who has reached a plateau in the company and is going nowhere may be resentful to any potential "comers" who might outdistance him. An insecure employee tends to be paranoid about those closing in on him. Nepotists are fearful of intruders on the family turf. Some professionals are concerned that the hiring of an aide for auxiliary duties will dilute the professionalism of the unit, and they would rather see these people placed in another department. The loners do not want to be disturbed.

GIVE IT TIME

The new employee should not judge these people too quickly. Some of them will "come around" in time; others will remain distant despite his best efforts. And sooner than he thinks, at least one helpful and supportive peer will probably emerge and lend a hand. Meanwhile, in guarding against making a poor impression, the new employee would do well to consider these potential bad-impression makers:

- Attitudes of cockiness and arrogance turn people off.
- The compulsive talker wears out his welcome. So does the smart aleck with his one-liners or off-color jokes.
- Indiscretion does not win friends; the one who is nosy and makes inquiries about the personal lives of others in the workplace is considered out of order.
- The new person who somehow always has an alibi for every error or misjudgment is shunned by his colleagues.
- The highly opinionated guy, who has views on everything from parenthood to the next invasion of Poland, tends to weary his colleagues and waste their time.

Newcomers to the workplace are strangers, in the sociological sense, and strangers are not readily taken into the tribal group. In the opening weeks the nature of their presence is established. Subsequently, they are either accepted, tolerated, or shunned. The final judgment is passed only after the new hire and the peers have done their posturing and sized one another up. The process

takes place quietly and the outcome is reached by un-
stated mutual consent. Then the parties either come close
or maintain distance. The relationship then proceeds at a
high, moderate, or low level of contact.

We try to attain acceptance, but until certain doubts are
removed, we settle for tolerance. Nobody wants to be
persona non grata; fortunately, even the person who is
generally distanced will in time probably find at least one
person in the large organization with whom he can be
comfortable.

The workplace is a testing ground. It tends to intensify
the question, "Will he or she be able to make it?"
Throughout this initial period (and probation) the new
employee is faced with the task of being able to cope: to
cope with himself, the job, his superior, other associates,
and with the work milieu in general. Often his or her career is at stake, or at least one leg on the journey to occupational or professional success. Economic survival
enters into it as well. No wonder the experience is an in-
tense one!!

Whether you are a new employee yourself or an "old
hand" looking at a new employee who has just entered
your workplace, try to follow these guidelines:

- Be sensitive
- Be aware
- Be confident and competent
- Be friendly

To underline all of the above, here's a wrap-up of constructive measures peers can take to help the new co-

worker feel at home, fit in, and be a better work partner. Give these a try.

The welcome greeting and a few words of conversation are more than just a gesture or nice things to do. Keep on doing them for every new man or woman who arrives.

Go on the assumption that *the orientation by the Personnel Department or the supervisor has its limits* and that nobody has as yet introduced the individual to the real culture of the organization, the personality of the company and what makes it tick. Proceed gradually to let him or her in on the corporate culture: how you dress, use the telephone prudently, call by first or last name, handle visitors, write memos, conduct yourselves at meetings, work with secretaries, go your respective ways to lunch, deal with vendors, handle the press, get a computer run priority, and a dozen other mores of your workplace. In essence, getting him or her to know the ropes and who's who.

Alert the newcomer to the boss's likes and dislikes, his insistence upon the right style (his style) of conduct. This preventive measure will spare him the hardship of finding out the innocent and costly way.

Pass the word quickly in regard to the company's reactions about a drink or two at lunch and returning with the smell of liquor, failing to attend a meeting, chronic lateness, missing the deadline for a report or a work project, encroaching on another person's decision-making turf, getting too chummy with one of the secretaries, or other sensitive action. In many companies, to ignore any one of these is to risk your reputation thereafter.

Every company has its code of ethics, written or unwritten. (Some companies have so poor a code of ethics they would rather not talk about it.) In either case, see that the new hire knows it promptly. Every organization also has some kind of institutional history—its origins, heroes, symbols of respect or status, alliances, stature within the industry, etc. Give him or her a brief history lesson.

Encourage, expedite, teach, support—in essence, do what you can to help your new co-worker adjust to the new environment and become productive early. Give him or her the chance to make good. However, do this within bounds of reasonableness.

Chapter 9

Picking Each Other's Brains

The chance to "pick brains" is a bonus that comes with the job . . . any job. If you haven't looked at it that way before, then do so now; the payoff can be substantial. Consider yourself fortunate if your co-workers have some special abilities on which you can draw now and then. They, in turn, should feel the same about tapping some of your special skills. It makes sense to capitalize on each other's assets. Among your peers and other co-workers there are probably a good number of brains available for picking. They can be tapped for many things: experience, ideas, special expertise, a sense of timing, and work habits.

FOR EXPERIENCES

Experience is a good guide, and it doesn't have to be your own experience; you can easily learn from someone else's. This is why we generally look with favor upon an old pro, a seasoned supervisor, a "veteran" employee who has been around and has learned from years of experience. What your co-worker has gained can be passed on, and you can be the beneficiary.

Ed Barlow lived through a strike that damaged his company three years ago, and remembers well the precautions taken by nonunion employees during that period of extreme tension and pressure—what to do, with whom it was safe to talk, how to deal with job interference, what to believe or disbelieve about the barrage of news flashes, and other lessons. With Ed's advice, current employees can lessen the risks of stepping on a boobytrap should another strike occur.

In another instance, one concerning the sensitivity of dealing with nepotism in the office, Helen Levin learned an important "tip" from the experiences of a peer. Her friend told her that a niece of the general manager would soon be transferred to Helen's department. Evidently, this was where all the newly hired family members began their careers. So, she was advised, it wouldn't be worth having a showdown with management if the niece's work performance was mediocre or her attitude indifferent.

In still another case one co-worker passed on to another valuable information about her experiences in handling "special" orders from an ill-tempered but long-standing customer.

Brain-picking, the timely transmittal of experiences encountered and lessons learned, is quite valuable. Use it wisely. Capitalize on your co-worker's experience in dealing with the internal company bureaucracy, in uncovering where the real sources of power and authority are located, or in getting an extension on an impossible deadline. Listen to some of the confirmed opinions about mixing sex and business in the work environment. You are likely to learn that in your company people are permitted informal, flirtatious, harmless sex talk and gesture, but that those who allow it to turn into serious affairs which disrupt family lives have had to pay dearly for it. The company is extremely harsh and unbending on this code. The co-worker's message to you: don't try it if you want to keep your job. That's the kind of lesson you learn from brain-picking and learning from the experiences of others. Neither seminar lectures nor canned training programs will yield such information. Only seasoned veterans of the workforce can impart such learning.

FOR IDEAS

One of the activities commonly shared on the job is to bounce thoughts off each other. You often hear this on the job: "Let me try this one on you; what if we were to do . . . ." This is another way of saying that we try to pick each other's brains for *ideas*, usually for the purpose of exploring something new, different, possibly creative. As producers and sellers of goods and services, we are on the alert as to how things can be improved or changed. "There is always a better way," Thomas Edison used to say in urging his associates toward more originality; eventually, this led to greater inventiveness. That better way may be a fresh approach toward making a process easier, quicker, and safer or a product better, more durable, and less expensive.

We do not project and share ideas that are visionary or born of fantasy; our colleagues do not wish to join us on Cloud Nine. At times we are theoretical, perhaps, but only where theory has a chance of being converted into practical application. Co-workers often come up with ideas that save the day. Many ingenious suggestions for change and improvement emerge in the workplace, frequently when you least expect them. Why, you wonder, had nobody thought of that before? Your co-worker's idea seems so timely, and its use can be tapped for the good of the operations and the people. Fertile ideas emerge in conversation about the job, at meetings, in the car pool, and while looking on curiously as other people work.

The clerk's mind finally clicked; there *was* a possible solution to her dilemma—an uncomfortable office jammed with many large metal file cabinets. Her co-worker in a large branch of this real estate firm had casually mentioned the notion of microfilming some of the contents of crowded file cabinets. Based on this suggestion the clerk and her superior conferred and decided to microfilm a large portion of records, correspondence, and documents dating back ten years or more. With the drastic reduction in old records now microfilmed, they were able to relieve the office of many metal files. The new space gained could be decorated with a two-cushion leather couch for visitors and floor vases with fully grown jade plants. For the first time, too, several Monet country-scene lithographs adorned the wall.

In a fabricating plant workers were now and then idled because of "downtime" due to lack of a particular raw material—a metal alloy used in preparing the cabin framework of yachts and other pleasure boats. A peer in the engineering department posed the idea of using plastic material as well as the metal, since either one would be acceptable. Now, if the inventory of one were to be low at any given time the company could use the other and thereby avoid any layoffs or production loss.

While at work in a pharmaceutical company, a chemist noted the success of the company in the development and sale of certain drugs for human consumption. He remarked to a co-worker in the lab that since the drugs worked so well for human medicine, why not try them for veterinary medicine? The idea caught the interest of other professionals and managers and, subsequently, led to a large international market of appropriate medical products to maintain the health of horses, mules, goats, and other animals in the underdeveloped agrarian countries in the world.

A supervisor faced with the burden of increasing paperwork bemoaned the lack of time to deal with his people. "Take for example this monthly safety report," he complained. "No sooner do I complete and submit it for one month than I'm faced with another for the next month." One day at lunch a peer offered the idea of questioning the Safety Director about the frequency of such reporting. The supervisor reasoned that it might well be worth a try. The issue was resolved some time later when a decision was made to change from a monthly to a quarterly report. It proved to be a happy outcome for this supervisor (and other supervisors as well), whose paperwork was now considerably reduced.

Shared ideas abound in the corporate environment and in nonprofit institutions. Recently, many new ideas have been put forth about how to conserve energy and cut costs in the workplace. In times of economic stress, co-workers have shared ideas about reducing overtime pay, sharing secretarial assistance on a scheduled basis, trimming the departmental budget, and eliminating traditional activities that had outlived their usefulness. The whole area of "job enrichment" is abundant in ideas about how to counteract boredom, monotony, and mental fatigue among workers in certain kinds of jobs and how to improve employee morale. The source of many of these fertile ideas is generally co-worker concern for the betterment of conditions in the workplace.

Ideas do not only generate practical solutions; they also animate the workplace. They produce a degree of excitement. Tap your partner for ideas that are fresh, productive, and workable. Set his or her wits to work, and your co-worker will do the same for you. Sooner or later, one of these ideas will turn out to be the catalyst to still more ideas and to proposals that eventually become practicable innovations. And do not be surprised to find in your brain-picking for ideas that a co-worker will come up with one that takes a poke at some sacred cow in the organization.

FOR EXPERTISE

A number of your peers have some *special expertise*. Research studies have confirmed that one of the key job satisfactions derived by peers is the feeling that other co-workers recognize their skills and call upon them for their special knowledge and expertise. Indeed, job satisfaction increases as they are able to pool and share knowledge. To be sure, there are also "poachers" in the organization who are ardently possessive of their own expertise and who remain aloof. They guard the knowledge zealously as a form of power and are reluctant to share it. Most companies cannot and often will not tolerate this arrogance for very long. Fortunately, such co-workers constitute only a small minority.

You will now and then tap your co-worker's brain for special knowledge, expertise, or mastery of a particular discipline. On one occasion you may call on her because she is a whiz at statistics. Perhaps the draft of the report you are writing needs to be reviewed by someone with mastery of statistical presentation. She will not look for errors or inaccuracies but for correct methodology, inferences drawn from the data, and verification of the main conclusions. With this help through brain-picking you could then proceed with the final version of the report and forward it more confidently. Or, in another instance you will call upon a co-worker for his special knowledge of product safety and liability. This information may persuade you to add another layer of insulation in the manufacture of the new electric stove—a safety precaution that could prevent a consumer or a dealer from suing your company.

You may also know a co-worker who is highly trained in graphics and graphic presentation. Tap that knowledge as best you can in preparing for a stand-up presentation of a proposal at a staff meeting or a management conference. Still another associate is gifted with mastery of the English language. As they say about him, "He has a way with words; the right word in the right place with the right punch." Maintain a good working relationship with this fellow. While he may not be available as your on-call editor, he will usually help you express a point differently, more tersely, or with greater clarity. Nudge him a bit more and he will even rephrase some points to give them the desired strong emotional appeal to sway the reader.

In increasing numbers people in the workplace are highly and technically educated in many specialized areas. Their brains can be picked for their special knowledge of metallurgy, computer science, nuclear power, cost accounting, quality control, labor-management relations, office management, health and safety laws, and other fields.

> A middle management official confided that she had "caught two big fish right here in the company waters" recently. One was an associate who practically helped her develop an entire survey strategy with full plans, questionnaire and interview techniques, and method of compiling results. (She had been delegated the task of launching a survey of employees in the company's twelve branches, focused on employee attitudes regarding selected personnel practices and career advancement opportunities for minority employees.) Her other discovery was a colleague who knew all the details of contract preparation—terminology, specifications, conditions for extension and renewal, and other essential information. Evidently he had been "in the contract game" for a number of years before transfer to his new duties here.

A supervisor, new on the job and assigned to the night shift, felt lost and isolated in the strange terrain. Within a few weeks he was faced with the need for some expertise about conducting a safety inspection after the installation of new equipment. There was no safety department on which to call. He also needed to know how to handle an incipient employee grievance, and there was no labor relations officer to be found. What did he do? He deliberately arrived at the plant three hours earlier than usual to buttonhole some knowledgeable people before they left at the end of the day shift. By picking their brains he was able to proceed correctly with both the safety inspection procedure and the employee grievance.

FOR SENSE OF TIMING

Good timing can be a key factor in winning acceptance or meeting defeat in job situations. It can also make the big difference between a sound move and an unwise risk. You should value good timing highly and brain-pick one or more of your co-workers who are known and respected for their good *sense of timing*.

The senior programmer thought he had ample time in which to complete his project plan, since the deadline was a month off. He felt he could safely put it aside for a while and turn his attention to other priorities. At a chance meeting with a colleague at lunch in the cafeteria, he was advised not to count too seriously on the agreed-upon deadline; the division director involved was known to change his mind and suddenly declare a new and shorter deadline. Several days later, word came from the director's office cutting the deadline from a month to slightly more than two weeks! Fortunately, the programmer was able to accelerate the pace and meet the new deadline—thanks to the timing suggested by his colleague. The chance meeting in the company cafeteria proved to be a very lucky break.

A shouting match erupted between the supervisor and a stock clerk in the warehouse. A buddy of the stock clerk urged him to get to the union steward immediately and claim that he had been threatened by the supervisor. This action was so well-timed that it placed the supervisor on the defensive; he withdrew a hastily drafted memo (about to be forwarded) which alleged insubordination on the part of the employee. Within two days an informal hearing resulted in dismissal of the entire incident, with no record. Had there been a delay, even of only a day or two, the insubordination charge would have been processed and disciplinary action against the employee invoked.

Women in a clerical group had complained for some time—to no avail—about headaches, work errors, and general discomfort because of inadequate lighting. At the initiative of one employee in the group, the women decided to insist upon new lighting fixtures immediately. Why? She argued that since the company had just hired a crew of carpenters to redo the older offices (walls, partitions, floors, windows, etc.) this would be precisely the right time to petition for new lighting fixtures in the ceiling. Her idea, with its good sense of timing, culminated a two-year effort to persuade management to install more modern lighting.

You have occasion, as most employees do, to "sweat it out" as the boss deliberates upon a memo, proposal, request, or a completed job which you had forwarded to him or her. There has been no response and you are now becoming concerned and restless. If you inquire, your action may be regarded as premature or overaggressive, and might indicate insecurity on your part; if you remain passive, your attitude may be viewed as lack of conviction or indifference. Moreover, the inaction could result in having the matter become "cold," and the boss might simply put it aside indefinitely. So you are in a squeeze, and the uncertainty and anxiety continue to build.

You also have occasion, as do many employees, to try to figure out what is the right time to have a face-to-face talk with the boss and ask for a raise, a change in responsibilities, or an earlier promotion. Apart from the merits of the case there is always the question of the best timing. If you feel that you know your boss's temperament and behavior or are able to predict his probable reaction, this will help your timing. If you are uncertain and puzzled, it may help to pick the brain of a savvy co-worker whom you can trust to keep your private efforts confidential. This co-worker or another may already have been through the same thing you are now experiencing and could be helpful in assessing the right time to take the next step.

Close co-workers can aid one another in suggesting a warning to an employee or take some other disciplinary action; they can decide the right time to put in bids for specific dates for summer vacation; they can also discourage the timing of certain actions that may smack of apple-polishing or appear inappropriate. In many cases they reinforce your desire to help a boss or an overloaded associate who is trying to handle five things the very week that some important company or trade event is being held. They may suggest the right timing so that he or she will not feel oversensitive about accepting a helping hand.

> Jeanette R. found the opportune time to confer with her superior about approval of a tuition-paid request for a course in consumer behavior. In truth she did not really "find" it; she was tipped off by a co-worker that this is the point in the fiscal year when budget estimates are prepared for employee benefits costs, including company coverage of tuition-paid courses. The approval went through. Had the request been made two weeks later, it would probably have been too late.

> Harry B., on the other hand, presented a request that was ill-timed. He saw the need for a brief trip to the Philadelphia branch to advise on the improvement of a new technical process. His boss barked an emphatic "No" on the phone. During the past month relationships between Philadelphia and the headquarters office had been very strained, even tense, because of a misunderstanding and a clash of personalities. There was need for things to cool off before a visitor from headquarters would be wel-

come. If Harry had had his ear to the ground he would have learned from some co-worker that trouble was brewing and that a trip at this point would be ill-timed.

Co-workers come to know, almost intuitively, what does *not* fit the occasion—when the timing is off. It is wrong timing, they contend, to try to get the attention of the repair shop on Thursday or Friday. By that time they are usually already booked for the full week, and to have the repair job done on Saturday will incur expensive overtime costs for the department. They know which bosses do not want to be cornered in the hallway for their views on a recent memorandum and which ones consider the hallway an appropriate place to discuss business. Co-workers seem to know, too, when the timing is off in regard to making friends or socializing with others. They seem to know, with unfailing intuition, which decisions are pending and which have already been made. Their advice on "waiting it out" until the timing is opportune has often saved an individual from the embarrassment of rushing into a decision or from making promises or commitments that could not be honored.

Cultivate your own sense of timing—it is an important part of your self-development—but don't hesitate to pick the brain of your co-workers (many of whom have undergone timing risks) and capitalize on their experience.

FOR WORK HABITS

Good skills and work habits are essential to overall performance. Our work habits reflect our use of time and energy and have a huge impact on our productivity. Employers have little use for those whose work habits are sloppy, careless, or wasteful or lead to negligence and hazard in the workplace. As serious workers we tend to observe our co-workers' *work habits* in action and react to what we see, positively or negatively. Much can be learned from observing good work habits, and we usually do more than just observe—we tend to talk about it. In essence, we try to brain-pick and consciously adopt the good work habits that we see and to avoid the bad ones.

In a blue-collar setting you observe how a co-worker attains quality and quantity performance. This has long been the way an apprentice, helper, or trainee learns from the senior, experienced journeyman. The skillful machinist, welder, fitter, or other artisan serves as a model for high marks on accuracy. The bottom line is little or no waste, spoilage, rejection, or need to redo the task. The master's habits of physical handling, movement, and concentration are worth observing, discussing, and adopting. So it goes, too, for work in an office setting, where secretaries, clerks, typists, filers, and others perform with unusual proficiency and skill.

In a professional and technical setting you note a co-worker's habits as he or she allocates duties for the day, reads technical material rapidly and with comprehension, drafts a technical report, verifies test results, finds access to needed library materials, and exercises professional courtesy. Activities vary, of course, among professionals in different functions—sales, public relations, market research, finance, or engineering—but good work habits are universal and consistently productive.

In a managerial setting work habits usually deal with people and programs—making appointments for the day, handling correspondence, following through on projects, checking for the control over operations, getting ready for meetings, delegating work to others, handling telephone calls, attaining better coordination with other departments, or planning ahead for the next week or month. In studying managerial work habits, you will observe how a manager deals with time, energy, people, and priorities and manages his or her emotions in the midst of all these activities.

Wherever you are in the workplace you will always be exposed to work habits, good and bad. Pick your co-workers' and peers' brains for their good work habits, and adopt those habits to the extent that you can. Imitating some of the habits or style of the good worker is not to be viewed as an indicator of one's own inadequacy. Rather, it is a deliberate way in which to do *better.* And don't worry that your co-workers will resent your picking their brains. Aren't *you* flattered when someone wants to learn from *your* experience?

While this chapter has been concerned with why, when, and how to brain-pick, a few comments must be made in regard to *whom* you brain-pick. Shun any attempt to ape anyone else's personality, temperament, likes, or dislikes. Avoid any deliberate effort to seek out a particular role model—the so-called smart operator, the fast-track and ambitious mover, the bureaucrat who knows his way around, or the corporate nepotist and loyalist who can put in a good word for you. Be yourself. Brain-pick the person with these assets: workplace maturity; sound judgment and discretion; willingness, within reasonable bounds, to share what he or she knows; and the respect of his peers.

Above all, pick the brains of the people you know, like, and respect. These are your friends—or your potential friends. Just as confiding in friends and helping them are routes to good office friendships, so is good brain-picking. Perhaps now is a good time to repeat the Stewart Syndrome: *To make it on your own, you will have to do it with or through others.*

Chapter 10

The Time You Spend Together

A work friendship doesn't just happen. Each partner has to give of himself or herself in time, effort, and energy. Just as you expect to put thought and emotion into an ongoing relationship, so you must also expect to allot some time toward building the friendship. Part of that time should be allocated to the sharing of work interests and part to pursuing personal interests.

In a major survey that focused on the various ingredients of friendship, more than 61% of the respondents cited "Willingness to make the time for me" as an important ingredient. Time—in some instances a substantial block of it—has to be invested to cultivate and sustain a friendship.

COMMUNICATION TAKES TIME

Your time is needed for these purposes:

- To confer and consult with your peers;
- To be available when a crisis occurs and your assistance may be needed;
- To listen, fully and attentively;
- To clarify a difference or a misunderstanding;

- To show concern in your work partner's problems and progress;
- To negotiate with or persuade your friend to accept an idea or a proposal;
- To explain, coach, interpret, in the best interests of doing the work better.

As you get to know your friend better, you'll find that there are further demands on your time. Your own sensitivity will alert you to your friend's needs, whether for advice, a friendly chat, or help with a project. Here are some tips for filling the basic and recurring needs that arise within the work friendship.

Get around to your peer's work site now and then; it's a way of showing concern. Even if you only drop by for a brief five-to-ten-minute visit in his office it gives evidence of genuine interest in how he's doing. Reassurance and reinforcement can be transmitted in even the briefest visit. Your friend will probably reciprocate. This investment in time will at some stage yield dividends in mutualism and good will. So make it a point to get around.

Be aware of the ups and downs in his job. Just as you encounter some rough spots in the course of the work week, so does your friend. He may be chasing around for certain statistics, data, or other information which for some reason appear to be elusive. He may run into a blank wall trying to procure a piece of equipment for several days' use. Certain preliminary tests just aren't working out as expected and so he cannot proceed with part of the subject. Maybe his colleague is on vacation and the backlog of work is putting undue pressure on the other employees in his department. You may or may not be able to help him over these rough spots, but the fact that you are available to listen and to share his concern is important. Perhaps he may want to put up a trial balloon and propose a new idea. Your presence now and then is very helpful to him. The time invested strengthens the relationship. Follow-up is an indicator of good will, so plan to follow up with a call.

Be sensitive to misunderstandings. Things don't always go smoothly in the relationship; time is often needed to heal major and minor wounds. One or the other of you may misconstrue a statement or become emotionally upset over a particular matter. A bit of rumor or gossip can annoy either or both work partners. However minor it may appear at the outset, an unpleasant incident tends to fester and the misunderstanding deepens. Take the time to nip it in the bud and to resolve the difference before it can become exaggerated and more hurtful. Be determined to find a time and place to talk privately and to give the problem the attention it needs. Isolation and avoidance are poor strategies.

Take the time to explain changes to a new system or some other complexity, so that your friend can understand it more clearly and promptly. Clarify a policy or a set of procedures if you think your friend would benefit, and go over any new content covered in a meeting if you sense that he needs some interpretation. Good peers do this for one another. They refer to the time spent as "coaching" time for each other.

Help him catch up after an absence. In a fast moving, dynamic organization an absence of several days from the office can put one far behind, whether the absence is for illness, travel, or jury duty. Whatever the case, for a good relationship personally and for desirable teamwork be sensitive to the importance of putting aside the needed time to fill in the gaps and keep your friend well informed. His own office staff can fill him in on the more urgent and immediate matters, but he may have missed one or two key meetings, overlooked the reading of some important report or paper routed to his in-basket, or fallen behind on some recent developments. As a good peer and friend, take the time to brief him and to make sure that he is currently informed.

Working together: Give it plenty of time. Perhaps the largest chunk of time you'll expend is in collaborating with one another. So many aspects of a plan and its execution are involved that you must count on spending a substantial amount of time. It is here that the questions of what, when, where, who, and how are resolved and that individual or joint actions can be agreed upon. Hurry or superficiality usually does not save time; indeed, it often results in the waste of time. Set aside generous blocks of time for effective collaboration. It will pay off in better coordination and more efficient handling of the project as well as making the process more pleasant.

Fun is important, too. Occasional socializing is an excellent use of your time. A pleasant social bond is important to a working relationship; finding the time for lunch, a game of table tennis, a "happy hour" after work in the nearby cafe, a long walk, or other get-together often improves the relationship. In some relationships where the work friendship has fully matured, the inclusion of spouses or mutual friends makes the socializing even more pleasant.

Be there when your friend needs you. A sense of responsibility or duty enters the friendship if you have to allocate time to visit your friend at home or in the hospital. If he is ailing and unable to be at work for a period, your patience and tolerance may be required in addition to your time, particularly if he has had a setback or a serious disappointment. Person-to-person empathy and long periods of listening and giving advice may be required of you. People often need access to a strong shoulder, a willing ear, a reassuring voice. Good friends learn the art of keeping on top of their own burden and still finding the time to listen to a close work-friend.

THE ART OF GOOD LISTENING

Time is more than a quantitative measure—minutes, hours, a morning, part of the week. It carries, too, a qualitative element. For quality results to accompany the time invested, especially among peers where most of the communication is oral, good listening is essential.

Listening is not as easy as you think. Often we believe that we are listening when we are merely hearing sounds and going through the motions of appearing to understand. *Real* listening involves full attention, sympathetic understanding, and critical evaluations.

Listen for the Meaning of the Words

One listens to more than words. As a listener you are subconsciously probing or looking *behind* the words. You try to ascertain what mood or attitude is expressed through these words, what feelings and emotions are generated by the speaker to accompany the mosaic of words. The mood or tone of what he has to say may be hopeful and constructive or it may be gloomy, negative, or even hostile. You evaluate as you listen, and your response depends on how you react to the attitudes that you perceive.

Take It All In, Sort It All Out

As you listen evaluatively, you will be "sizing up" the speaker. You know a certain amount about the character and reputation of your co-worker; his past promises and actions form a base on which you have judged his character, and what he has to say now will be influenced by what you already know. You feel that he is a person of integrity and can be trusted fully; he has always shown intellectual honesty in presenting both the pros and cons of an issue, and you respect this characteristic. As a listener you are also influenced, perhaps, by his position or his associates in the company: he is known to have an "in" with the more influential executives, or he is known to fraternize with and to be accepted by the vice-president for marketing. In the case of a younger person, he or she may be regarded as a "hot-shot," destined to rise rapidly in the organization. Perhaps you are aware of the speaker's faults; she is known to be a gossip, or a betrayer of confidences. In this case you really do not listen at all, or you listen with a degree of built-in caution. Sizing up the speaker may be well and good, but do guard against prejudging a person to the extent that you may miss the real message because of your prior opinion. Listen *carefully*.

Your Own Needs May Be a Barrier

You may be influenced by your own needs and characteristics as you listen and this may distort the communication. As a listener, the extent to which you do or do not possess an adequate body of knowledge or information affects your listening. Your habits of thinking make a difference. Your psychic needs at the time—to feel important, to belong, to unload some discontent—affect your reception of what is said or discussed. Your aspirations, beliefs, and convictions also affect the way you hear new ideas. Because of your own needs or characteristics you may at times be poorly equipped to accurately and fully decode the message which is being presented. Be aware of your own response.

Atmosphere Makes a Difference

Surely, the setting will influence your listening capability. The time and the place are clearly important factors. Whether the exchange is just between you and your peer or in the presence of a large number of people makes a difference in the attentiveness and in the time that can be given to the dialogue. The tone of the environment is also a factor: when everything is in a state of panic and the place seems like a pressure-cooker, it is difficult to listen logically or attentively; when things are calm and departments function at their normal pace, the prospects for better listening are considerably improved.

Guidelines for Even Better Listening

Since you are investing your time in a friendship that has value for you, you would do well to spend some of it improving your listening techniques. Here are some guidelines:

- Judge the *content* rather than the speaker himself. Focus on what he knows and whether these are pieces of information you should also know.
- Be alert to the central idea being conveyed and not necessarily to all the details. Facts can be filled in or confirmed later.
- Hold your fire. Avoid being too eager to find holes or to criticize. Let the full message unfold first, and some of the premature criticism will probably be rebutted.
- Withhold your favorable evaluation as well; that, too, may be premature. Being aroused to quick enthusiasm is likely because of the excitement of an original idea or a fresh viewpoint. Be restrained; modify as you go along.
- Stretch your mind as you listen to an exposition which is quite technical, complex, and perhaps tough to comprehend. Deliberate stretching seems to assure the needed attentiveness. If you have to take notes during an explanation, do it in shorthand and do it quickly so that you can return to the listening role as soon as possible before some of the content is missed.
- Voice change, hand gestures, facial expressions, eye contact, physical movements in sitting or standing— these and other nonverbal signs are often as telling as the words. To get the full impact of what the

speaker seeks to transmit, be sure to listen and watch for the verbal and the nonverbal parts of the communication. Emotions, particularly, are conveyed by the physical gestures. Be alert to interludes of silence.

- Encourage the speaker to go on by means of some eye contact of your own—a nod of assent, a "carry on" comment, or other means of showing interest and attention.

- Ward off distractions such as noise or interruptions which interfere with concentration. Check out the window, door, the telephone, possible visitors, etc., to assure sustained and concentrated listening.

- Do some mental questioning as you go along; weigh the evidence. Ask yourself about the statistics, illustrative points, and facts as he continues. Are they accurate? What is their source? Do these tell the full story or is he distilling what he wants in order to prove his point? This is part of the evaluation. Listen to what is *unsaid* as well as to what is said.

- Avoid becoming upset by words that offend you— "damn," "has-been," "watchdog," "bureaucrat," "dame," "chiseler," or four-letter words of profanity. You may be developing a "deaf spot" because of their use and thereby miss the main content of what is being said. You can let him know afterward if you resent his choice of language.

- If you are able to anticipate what the person is going to say next, do so. In this way you can tick off one key point at a time.

- Listen broadly as well as deeply. Be prepared to listen to a wide range of matters in the workplace: the petty gripes and the large issues; the commonplace items and the highly technical projects; good news

and bad news; fresh ideas and old-fashioned salesmanship; rumors and truths; ego inflation and larger
company interests, or personal values and corporate
values; words of genuine negotiation and words of
threat. Do your best to be objective, attentive, and
flexible as you take the role of listener. It *is* an art;
you will do well to master it.

GUIDELINES FOR INVESTING YOUR TIME

In order to be accessible—to get around to see others,
confer with others, listen well, resolve a difference or misunderstanding, and show concern or assist your peer—
you must manage your own time well. Learn to conserve
time, to control time, and to utilize time effectively.
Here's how:

- Budget your week so as to have time allocated for
  your desk, your programs, and your circle of related
  people. Peers are to be seen, not just identified in
  the organizational chart boxes.
- Take care of your priorities. Deferred decisions and
  procrastination only make things worse. Once you
  are on top of your priorities, you have some margin
  of discretionary time to get around and see people.
- Plan to drop by and see a colleague once every week
  or two; do it with regularity. If you cannot make it at
  a particular time, telephone or send a friendly memo
  to indicate that you will try to make it next time.
- Improve your capability as a planner. The unplanned
  or poorly planned office encounters too many crises
  which encumber you and drain away your time.
- When the hour or more of collaborating proves to be

a productive session, take a moment to call your peer and tell him it was time well invested. He may feel the same way about it.

- Guard against becoming a workaholic. Invest time to socialize now and then with a peer: attend a ballet, get tickets for the basketball game, or make a date to go jogging together. Or, plan to visit and see how he prunes an azalea shrub or she does a piece of sculpture and then stay for a cup of coffee and conversation.
- Simplify your paperwork; try to eliminate as much nonessential paper as you can. There's no joy in massaging paper. It's more fun stroking people.
- Watch the time robbers—the extended telephone calls, reports, unexpected visitors, excessive meetings, those incidents which provoke complaints and grievances, inaccessible records, worthless reading, and other items that drain your time. The time you gain can be spent more profitably elsewhere.
- Utilize the computer for rapid retrieval of information. It should then free you for time needed on other matters. Don't be victimized by years of habit doing things the old way, usually the longer and more tedious way of processing information.

INTERLOCKING

There is a strong correlation among these three: managing your job, managing your peer friendships, and managing time. Investing time to build and sustain fine friendships with your peers is an investment that pays off well.

An interview with an automobile plant foreman brought forth this time-management pattern:

Every morning I spend one hour reviewing our production and quality control reports of the previous day. Then I scan the accident and injury reports, and finally the "GCG" (gripes/complaints/grievances) summary. As may be necessary I then delegate to the assistant foreman the task of following up on safety or employee relations items. By 10 a.m. I am through, and I spend the rest of the morning going from one shop to another just visiting with the people, talking, inquiring, answering questions, and giving them whatever advice and encouragement I can. The time invested has made us a far better team here.

Few of us can find the time to do this daily, but we can and should devise a pattern and a plan for spending time with our office friends. It takes time to build and strengthen relationships and to make them satisfying and productive.

How Good a Friend Are You?

Before going on to read about the problems and pitfalls of workplace relationships, stop for a moment and complete the following questionnaire.

WINNING RELATIONSHIPS PROFILE

This is a self-audit of how you tend to relate to co-workers, work jointly on projects with them, face work problems, collaborate, and compete. It also reveals the level of your ability to maintain effective peer relationships.

Based on research and experience in behavioral science and interpersonal relations, the statements reflect responses that are "most acceptable," "generally acceptable," or "least acceptable." They are not "right" or "wrong" answers.

Read each situation and the related series of three statements. Enter an X mark next to the statement that indicates your view most closely.

At the close of the self-audit you will find the scoring key. By using this key against your responses you will arive at a total score. The total score and range, based on your responses, will reveal a profile of your working relationships with peers.

SITUATIONS

1. When a change is proposed in the work setting, I tend to be . . .
   a. ☐ resistant, prefer to hold to the status quo;
   b. ☐ skeptical, but willing to go along if convinced of the need for it;
   c. ☐ agreeable and ready to listen and participate in the change.

2. The morale of my immediate work group (superior, coworkers, etc.) . . .
   a. ☐ generally affects my own morale and work performance, and I do what I can to keep group morale high;
   b. ☐ has its ups and downs, and leaves me somewhat neutral;
   c. ☐ doesn't influence me much at all in getting the job done.

3. Regarding the flow of information at work, I tend to . . .
   a. ☐ judge each situation and act accordingly in sharing information;
   b. ☐ be rather guarded, seldom exchange information unless required;

c. ☐ share information quite often and willingly with others at work.

4. As for seeking or having acceptance and approval of my co-workers . . .
   a. ☐ I am almost always aware of it and seek this recognition;
   b. ☐ now and then I expect it as the situation warrants;
   c. ☐ I really don't care much about it.

5. When a mistake is made be me or by a work partner . . .
   a. ☐ I tend to overreact, exaggerate the incident, blame my-self or others;
   b. ☐ feel badly, but try to learn from it and get on with the show;
   c. ☐ just "cover up" and do the task over again—this time correctly.

6. My tolerance level in dealing with a co-worker's annoying mannerisms is . . .
   a. ☐ generally high;
   b. ☐ moderate;
   c. ☐ generally low.

7. I believe that it is most difficult to have a personal rela-tionship with . . .
   a. ☐ your peer or work partner;
   b. ☐ your boss;
   c. ☐ your subordinate.

8. If the need arises to be critical of a co-worker, it is my style . . .
   a. ☐ to be straightforward and criticize the individual directly;
   b. ☐ to criticize the action or result rather than the person;

c. ☐ to be more cautious in the future in dealing with this person's work product, but I say nothing about it.

9. Consulting and conferring with others . . .
a. ☐ is generally a waste of time, although this is expected of me;
b. ☐ will lead to a useful idea or method now and then, but I have to be persuaded that it's worth the time and effort involved;
c. ☐ is a very good approach, since problems are becoming more complex and unilateral judgment is likely to be inadequate or risky.

10. When I have a new or innovative idea, I would rather . . .
a. ☐ test it out by exploring it with my peers and get their feedback;
b. ☐ present it to my superior, in a one-to-one conference, for adoption;
c. ☐ keep it to myself and spring it on the right person at the right time, hoping for some recognition or reward.

11. When listening to another person at work I usually . . .
a. ☐ prefer to "shoot the breeze" and try to shun serious talk as much as possible;
b. ☐ cut it off once I have the essential facts and the main point;
c. ☐ try to listen not only to the facts but also to his views, feelings, and concern about the matter—to listen evaluatively.

12. I perceive myself to be . . .
a. ☐ generally an active, team-oriented person;
b. ☐ an independent worker, for the most part;

c. ☐ a team person when the nature of the work project requires it.

13. In regard to "breaking in" the new employee, my reaction is . . .
   a. ☐ I'm concerned that he or she will "eat into my time" with questions, interruptions, seeking information, etc.;
   b. ☐ it's the supervisor's problem to "break in" new people, not mine;
   c. ☐ every employee deserves a chance to make good in adapting to the new environment, and if I can help occasionally I'll gladly do it.

14. Coping with problems is not easy, and I tend to . . .
   a. ☐ talk it over with a colleague or work friend in the workplace;
   b. ☐ blow off steam; take it out on others;
   c. ☐ keep it to myself, and immerse myself more deeply in work.

15. A personality clash can occur between two co-workers, and when it does I . . .
   a. ☐ delay taking any action, and for the present just go about my work;
   b. ☐ am not willing to give in;
   c. ☐ am generally ready to resolve the disagreement early because it is apt to deepen if left unresolved.

16. In trying to reach agreement with others on a problem, I believe in . . .
   a. ☐ defending your position as persuasively as possible, but being ready to bend or compromise if your view should not prevail fully;

b. ☐ holding your ground; never yield once you've taken a position on the matter;

c. ☐ being open to various alternatives, since one of these is likely to turn out as agreeable and acceptable.

17. Cliques often try to influence things, and my reaction is . . .

a. ☐ don't tolerate their interference; confront them if you have to;

b. ☐ try to avoid them; they're trouble;

c. ☐ they're here to stay; try to understand their function and to work with them as well as you can, in the best interests of company progress.

18. If a co-worker does something wrong (i.e., faked absence, drinking or gambling on the premises, deliberate error, etc.), I tend to . . .

a. ☐ level with him privately that his job could be in jeopardy and try to have him correct his ways;

b. ☐ let other co-workers, who usually know about it, take over and spread rumor or "blow the whistle" on him;

c. ☐ detach myself as completely as possible from this person.

19. When I compete with others for a promotion or other reward, here's how I view it . . .

a. ☐ I'll let my performance record and potential speak for itself;

b. ☐ I'll do anything that I can to beat him, even if it seriously impairs our personal relationship afterward;

c. ☐ I believe in healthy rivalry and I want to win, but if I lose I must be prepared to restore a good working relationship with him.

20. When a co-worker and I have had our joint project rejected or shelved I prefer to . . .
   a. ☐ confer, revive it, and improve on it for eventual acceptance;
   b. ☐ throw in the towel;
   c. ☐ express disappointment (and possibly some resentment) to our boss and ask for an explanation for the turndown.

SCORING KEY—AND ANSWERS

1 point for the *least* acceptable; *2* points for the *generally* acceptable; and, *3* points for the *most* acceptable statement/answer.

Situation	"least"	"generally"	"most"
1	a. ____	b. ____	c. ____
2	c. ____	b. ____	a. ____
3	b. ____	a. ____	c. ____
4	c. ____	b. ____	a. ____
5	a. ____	b. ____	c. ____
6	c. ____	b. ____	a. ____
7	b. ____	a. ____	c. ____
8	a. ____	c. ____	b. ____
9	a. ____	b. ____	c. ____
10	c. ____	b. ____	a. ____
11	a. ____	b. ____	c. ____
12	b. ____	c. ____	a. ____
13	a. ____	b. ____	c. ____
14	b. ____	c. ____	a. ____
15	b. ____	a. ____	c. ____
16	b. ____	a. ____	c. ____
17	b. ____	a. ____	c. ____
18	c. ____	b. ____	a. ____

19 . . . . . b. _____ a. _____ c. _____
20 . . . . . b. _____ c. _____ a. _____
Total _____ Total _____ Total _____
Grand total _____

YOUR TOTAL SCORE—AND PROFILE

If your score is under 40, you have a LIMITED work relationships profile. If you scored 41–50, you have a MODERATE work relationships profile. If you scored 51–60, you have a HIGH work relationships profile.

Use the result of this self-audit for your continued personal growth in working, cooperating, and competing with co-workers. The guidelines in this book will enable you to improve your interpersonal skills and to become a more effective peer collaborator.

Part Three

Weathering the Storms

With light there is shadow; with energy there is fatigue. So, with the asset of having the pillar of a peer there is also the prospect that some day that pillar may become unsteady and may even crumble. Cracks may weaken the structure. The strains and stresses of events may conceivably cause its collapse.

Misunderstanding, disagreement, and personal competitiveness may arise in the course of the peer relationship. Problems of one kind or another and stressful situations or events should be taken seriously, especially the major ones. As a mature worker, you need to understand what some of these critical situations might be and to anticipate that they could happen to you and your co-worker.

This part of the book deals with some of the major storms that may be encountered in a working friendship and how best to weather them.

Chapter 11

The Changing Workplace

The workplace changes as the composition of the nation's workforce changes. You can expect to find many different kinds of people thrust together in a typical work site. Men and women, young and old, white and black, rural and urban people, the physically able and the handicapped, some affluent and others of modest means, the barely literate or the well-educated, and workers on full-time or part-time basis are in the workforce. Among them are the highly experienced and the beginners, one-income and two-income family members, the natives and the newcomers. This is a far cry from the simple way in which we used to classify employees: union or nonunion, permanent or temporary, white collar or blue collar.

THE NEW DIVERSITY

No longer is there a clear distinction between professional and nonprofessional, for there has been a proliferation of paraprofessional, technical, subprofessional, and administrative employees working more and more closely with the professionals. They expect separate recognition and status. The profiles of married and single employees are not easily drawn. "Single" may mean an employee separated, divorced, widowed, or living with another, rather than solely one who has never married. The personal and home responsibilities, and the career aspirations, of the "singles" may be as great as those of the "marrieds," and their stresses of coping with home and job are not dissimilar.

Part-time workers are becoming more common in many companies. Estimates range from 1½ to 2 million part-time workers, either by choice, availability, or company need to reduce payroll expenses. This is quite a change, since part-time employment had been frowned upon and resisted for a number of decades. Part-timers and temporaries are now welcome.

In fact, you will find more differences than similarities in your co-workers: differences in age, sex, religion, ethnic background, geographic roots, habits, and economic status. But there is one main similarity that binds all of you together: the company has, through its selection process, hired a qualified person with the skills and capability to perform the job well, or who can be trained to perform well and become productive quickly.

As the diversity of workers widens, so does the range of temperament among co-workers. You seldom have the option of choosing them, and they may not have the kind of "chemistry" to blend with yours. Their mannerisms may not be quite what you would like or what you have been brought up to expect. They make poor lunch partners because of incessant gab, have an odd accent, repeat the same old stories, or observe religious holidays you've never heard of. You may encounter co-workers who are excessively withdrawn, who smoke foul-smelling pipes, or who are subtly critical of everything.

No matter how hard you try—even if you are one of those who believe in "forgetting" the office the minute you leave it—you cannot totally separate your personal life from your working life. We carry our emotions from one part of our life to the other, and they can't be conveniently hidden or forgotten for a number of hours each day. Temperament, habits, personality traits are difficult to conceal; they have a way of emerging as people react to their environments. Some workers are quick to anger while others have remarkable patience.

The new diversity in the working world requires a new understanding and a new strategy for coping. You'll be more comfortable if you can develop a high level of tolerance and acceptance of the workplace and its people. You'll need that tolerance and that patience if you are to feel truly comfortable in today's—and tomorrow's— changing workplace.

The new diversity brings not only a wider variety of backgrounds and types of worker, but also several more specific kinds of "newcomers."

More Older Workers . . .

A higher proportion of older workers—those past sixty— now choose to remain in their jobs. Reductions in and taxation on the social security benefits prevent many older workers from making ends meet on just these benefits and a modest company pension. They will defer retirement and continue on the job until age 68, 69, or 70 rather than retiring at 65 or sooner. Inflationary health-care costs (hospital, medication, physician and dental costs, etc.) for elderly workers create such economic uncertainty that they feel more secure staying on the job additional years.

And More Younger Ones

Demographically, during this decade the largest increase in the workforce will be in the 25–44 age group; an increase of more than 14 million workers in this age group, more or less equally divided between men and women is expected. This group promises better work relationships between men and women in the workplace; they are neither too young to be gullible nor too old to be rigid. Attributes of more-willing accommodation and flexibility are important assets that characterize this age group.

More Women

A marked change will also be noted in regard to those in positions as foreperson, supervisor, manager, administrator, or executive. Women will increasingly occupy these positions. Consider this trend: in 1960 women managers numbered just more than 1 million; a surge took place and increased this considerably by 1970; and by 1980 they approached nearly 3 million in managerial jobs. The growth was more than 180 percent, versus 37 percent for men during this twenty-year period. Moreover, there has been remarkable growth in the number of women in the professions; and, as the college enrollment of women rises and they enter upon careers in business, law, science, journalism, etc., they will correspondingly occupy later many more managerial and administrative positions within these professions.

We will soon have a workforce that is divided equally between men and women. This will culminate a trend of the past twenty years and one that is still accelerating remarkably fast. Of all women in the workforce, numbering about 44 million, about 20% are single, 56% married, and 24% divorced, separated, or widowed. Unfortunately, of the women who are heads of the household one in three earns so little money as to be living at or below the poverty level. The pay gap is still notoriously wide. You may encounter attitudes of resentment in the workplace because of this inequity.

New Technology

Technologically, too, the workplace is changing at a swift pace. More and more automated equipment and procedures invade the office and the plant. Word processing is destined to alter the way in which co-workers perform office work in preparing copy, filing, record-keeping, communicating, and transmitting information. Increased use of computers in all facets of business, industry, and government will affect worker skills, habits, and relationships.

WHAT ALL THIS MEANS
A New Kind of Sharing

Topics of conversation among co-workers change with the increase of two-career couples whose children are entrusted to day-care facilities. Co-workers are increasingly discussing and sharing personal and family concerns. Company-paid tuition as a benefit for employees is a frequent subject. Career-oriented employees seek retraining and college degrees in order to qualify for upgrading to higher positions and better earnings. Continuing education becomes a pivotal concern. Getting ahead and achieving success in the workplace while trying to manage the combined stresses of home and job is also discussed more openly. Comparable worth, now focused on as a possible solution to pay disparity between the sexes, is gaining wide interest. Parenting becomes a more frequent topic of conversation. Difficulties related to hours of work, shifts, schedules, overtime, and travel become more pronounced as they affect parents' availability to their children. A growing interest is noted, among employees and their companies, in taking a day off when a child is sick at home. Child-care arrangements, in general, will preoccupy the attention of many.

Singleness, separation or pending divorce, and the troubles encountered in coping with aging parents often prompt people to seek a willing ear. A trusted work-friend may well offer this outlet. We may witness a stronger tendency for peers to share some of their personal strains as we work together. The art of making and keeping work friends will take on greater credibility than in the past.

Cutbacks: A Major Cause of Anxiety

Finally, we should not understate the seriousness of mergers, recessions, and other events. They leave scars on the workplace. Shockwaves of employee layoffs, furloughs, and freezes have severe bad effects. Anxiety continues to pervade the workplace and job jitters are still widespread. Personal dislocations and tragedies of co-workers are so vivid as to affect deeply those still employed. Be sensitive to the prevailing mood. Anticipate in some companies a setting of worried workers and lowered morale. Good peer relations, in such cases, will test your human qualities.

New Kinds of Problems

Unfortunately, the workplace has to be monitored. Too many people in the community are or will probably become habitual users of alcohol or drugs. This is a social problem of epidemic proportion which has spilled over into the workplace. Billions are spent annually to assist addicted employees, from educational programs warning against driving or handling equipment on the job while drunk or high to psychiatric and rehabilitation services for the chronic user of alcohol or drugs. In the workplace drug use is reported in surveys to have been directly involved in everything from train wrecks by marijuana-smoking trainmen to the removal of nuclear-power-plant engineers by state police for using amphetamines, marijuana, and other drugs. Reports disclose that cocaine use doubled among those over age 26 in the three-year period from 1979 to 1982. These are not kids on a school lark but mature adults at work. Many of these employees are entrusted with key responsibilities for the safety of people and property within the company's quarters. Even when these workers manage to perform reasonably satisfactorily on the job they are nevertheless prone to emotional stress, nervousness, and repeated absence because of illness.

A New Kind of Friendship

The effects of the changing workplace will certainly be felt in the more private and personal sphere of employee friendships. Cliques and groups will continue to form, as they always have, but they may contain more various kinds of people; they may reflect the diversity of the workplace. This is all to the good, provided that employees are prepared for the changes and receptive to them.

Rigidity will seriously impair one's ability to meet the new kind of friendship. Workers will need to be flexible, broadminded, and adaptable in tomorrow's workplace. Awareness of these changes, and a vow to meet the new scenarios head-on, is the healthiest way to begin.

Chapter 12

Rivalry –
When Peers Compete
for the Same Job

It's fair to say that practically everyone who has a job aspires to move up the ladder. Advancement brings many rewards—more prestige, more money, greater self-esteem, increased recognition, and probably more opportunities in the future. The pursuit of advancement introduces rivalry into the workplace. The higher you go in the organizational pyramid, the fewer positions or openings there are available. Not only is there little room at the top, but room is also limited even in the middle and lower echelons. Co-workers are thrust into competition when a position becomes available and they vie for the occasional opening that represents a promotion. Such competition between workers can be straightforward or sordid, depending upon the situation and the people involved.

Of course, employees are always jockeying for position. They try to attain more visibility in the eyes of their superiors, they seek approval, and they hope to be favored openly or subtly. Competing for a promotion intensifies this effort. For many an employee, failing to get the promotion can lead to severe frustration. Such an employee views nonpromotion as a sign of having reached the optimum level in his present job; there's no place to go and nothing to hope for in this organization. Consequently, a great deal is at stake as one competes with the other.

DIFFERENT SCENARIOS

The general view of rivalry has been that it brings out the worst in people and it convulses the workplace. Assertiveness, toughness, and manipulation can make the office a very unpleasant place. Some contend that if ambition is unbounded and unrestrained, mayhem can occur. It is further asserted that as the adversaries line up, so cliques and coalitions form to give their respective backing to either one. A healthy rivalry has turned into a cutthroat personal feud. One party or the other is likely to threaten to get even or to quit if the outcome is unfavorable. Rumors fill the corridors. Confrontation brings more tension. The notion prevails that at this point people talk in whispers and that each contender is constantly looking over his shoulder, apprehensive that some dirty trick is about to be pulled. No doubt there is some truth in this; competition for certain positions at certain levels can become ruthless.

However, interviews with many workers and personnel directors reveal another scenario. In interviews of both "winners" and "losers" in companies, the following statements were voiced indicating a mood that is quite different.

> "Many want to win in the competition but they
> won't be brutal about it. They're as much concerned

with their personal reputation as with the possible promotion."

"We're not out to get Phil or Edna or any other competing co-worker—but to get the *job*."

"It has been our experience here that candidates for the promotion go about it with seriousness but never with malice."

"We find the few contenders for the job to be evenly matched for the most part. So they know the selection made isn't based on loyalty to the company, years of service, experience, or other general factors. What they discovered is that the company is well aware of the past but is gearing up for the *future*, and so it looks for unusual potential of some specific important asset such as being more innovative, bolder in making decisions, or better attuned to the service aspects of the business. Those who don't get the promotion seem to settle for the fact that they lack that one asset management seeks as it turns to the future."

"This is the second time I've lost out. In fact, the two people who beat me subsequently became my bosses. I'm convinced they had more on the ball than I did and that they deserved the promotion."

"I could tell you a number of things about this company that are not commendable; but when it comes to picking people for promotion, I feel it is on the up-and-up. Most people here will agree on this subject."

"Our so-called career development program is a joke. I don't know anyone who has moved ahead because of this program. But the Personnel Department has done a first-rate job in helping people who have been passed over for promotion. The transfers, changes in assignment, opportunities for more supervisory and technical training, and other things done by Personnel have removed much of the usual bitterness that comes when people are passed over."

"Frankly, it hurt when a woman beat me and got the promotion. But now that it's over I must say that Adele Leavitt is a remarkable teacher as well as a very competent chemist. She has taught me and the others so much this past year that we're convinced management put her in the right place at the right time."

"If you don't try you'll never know what you're capable of, and so I compete whenever I think I'm qualified to be a contender. They encourage you to do it here, and someday I may actually make it. Most of my buddies here have a good attitude about it and that's good for morale."

These and other experiences testify to the fact that there's another side to the competition story. Both aspects are probably true, the bad and the good. Office politics and the exercise of power can lead to abuse. Yet, most individuals still have integrity and a sense of fair play as they compete.

REALITIES OF WORKPLACE COMPETITION

In a sound organization, healthy competition among peers brings out the best in employees' potential and capabilities. In an unsound organization it brings out the worst of human traits and organizational intrigue.

Emotions run high; alliances and coalitions often break up. Most peers go through the pangs of disappointment when they lose out, and some experience deep bitterness. But in the long run they recover and try again. Somehow maturity and good sense prevail in the end, and co-workers as rivals manage to restore their relationship with civility and get on with the show.

Workplace "intelligence" and awareness are essential to your prospects as a competitor. Knowing some of the "facts of life" about such competition is helpful. More than a philosophical shrug of "you win some, you lose some" is involved. You deal in strengths. A most significant fact is this: when the competition is over, win or lose, *the relationship between the two co-workers needs to be reconstructed or sustained*. In many cases neither gets the promotion: it goes to a third person elsewhere in the company or even to an outsider. In any event, renewing the co-worker relationship, when the rivalry is over, could prove to be an easy task or a difficult one depending upon your perspective and how things were handled during the competition.

Remember, too, that the company itself induces competitiveness. Management holds the view that individuals must stretch beyond their normal capacity if they wish to reach for the brass ring. Such reasoning also holds that internal competition impels workers to put forth their best effort, taps the latent abilities of teams of workers, and brings forth the full energies of the people. If this is done sensibly and without threatening overtones, management can often realize greater individual or team productivity and sometimes more imaginative approaches to problem-solving. It draws upon recognition as a motivator. The recognition may take the form of a pat on the back, a letter of commendation, a bonus, or some other form (often just short of a promotion) that puts the individual in a more favorable position if and when a promotion opportunity should arise. The point is that willy-nilly you are in a milieu of competitiveness even if you do not have high aspirations.

Other things must also be recognized for a better perspective on competition in the workplace. Some of these are mentioned next.

Some companies have very lax standards. Several employees in a company expressed what is symptomatic in a number of organizations: "Unless I screw something up badly and it becomes known, I'll be promoted on a regular basis up to a certain point." Surveys disclose that quite a number of workers perceive neutralism to be their most common behavior—neither too cooperative nor too competitive.

New areas of competition are to be found, notably generated by women who seek to enter the nontraditional jobs as well as the traditional. These include positions in the trades (electrician, miner, construction worker, etc.), in the services (security, safety inspection, fire-fighting, etc.), and in levels of management (foreperson, superintendent, floor manager, division vice-president, etc.) as more women seek more opportunities. Affirmative action considerations in promotability are written into the labor laws, and companies must comply or face penalties.

The two-income family has become part of the work culture, so that one spouse need not be dependent on the other for a promotion to further the family's economic status. Each can and does seek advancement on his or her own.

Merit pay increases and performance appraisals have lost their punch in many companies, unfortunately. In too many instances mediocre performers attain the same extra pay or higher rating as do the superior ones.

Mentorism in the workplace can be viewed as a boon or a bane. Mentors tend to become official or unofficial sponsors. Sometimes they do more than teach, guide, or counsel. They open doors to opportunities, influence, higher-ups in the organization, entrust their protégés with inside information, procure special assignments for them, and help them attain higher visibility. Does this introduce inequity in the promotion process? Some unsponsored people think so, particularly when they are seeking and competing against somebody's protégé for a certain promotion slot. Old boys' networks and the newer women's networks, as support groups within the company and in the industry, can unduly influence promotions.

Promotions are not always time linked. Business management consultants have observed that some employees naively approach advancement as a college junior who by next year will likely become a senior or a sergeant in the military who can well assume that within a year or two he will be promoted to the rank of master sergeant. Such time-linked concepts are applicable only to a limited extent in business and industry, where the usual linkage is keyed to economic prosperity of the company or to the availability of an opening. Those who just wait and count on an eventual promotion through sheer patience or durability are often grievously disappointed. Does company or institutional loyalty pay off? Not on this attribute alone. Experience indicates that a worker cannot depend upon loyalty alone to see him through the paths of promotion.

Probably one of the most vivid realities is that *opportunities for promotion are often quite uneven* in the company. While one division or department is expanding, another may be shrinking. A new contract gained may generate a number of opportunities in the engineering department but very few in the research unit. This year's budget may result in numerous promotion opportunities in the field branches but none at headquarters. A breakthrough enables the Marketing Division to open new territories and create five new sales managers but no managerial openings in the computer center. In short, expansion is generally not company-wide. The lesson for a number of aspirants is this: be alert as to where the action is and you may have more opportunity to put your competitive assets to work.

NEGATIVES DIM THE PROSPECTS

Some of the realities are quite distressing, sometimes even demoralizing to would-be contenders for a promotion.

Nepotism is one of these frustrations. The company, usually a smaller company, is comprised of family members and nonmembers. Since the family members are bound to the godfather, usually the president or vice-president of the company, they are among the favored and are heirs to the most prestigious and the best-paying positions. The nonmembers, considered valuable to the company but nevertheless outsiders, generally hold the run-of-the-mill positions. In the event of a vacancy in a highly regarded position the nonmember's chances for the promotion are very slim if the rival is one linked to the godfather. No matter how hard you try in such a company, only the lesser rewards will come your way. The real promotions will elude you.

Another dilemma is the company tactic of *compensatory award*. It is in effect a form of appeasement. Since you cannot get the promotion for some reason the company will make it up to you in some other way—a stock option, more generous pension plan, the use of a company car, more life insurance, or some other inducement for you to stay on. None of these compensatory awards, however, really fulfill the main motivations for your seeking earned advancement.

Particularly shattering is the *confidential "tip" that the promotion is all sewed up*. The tip usually proves to be true. Management goes through the charade of making it seem like a bona fide race among the several candidates but behind the scenes the decision has already been made to promote Joe.

Only slightly less traumatic is *the decision to fill the post with someone from the outside* on the ground that none of the contenders within the company is sufficiently qualified. At times this may well be a valid reason but in far too many cases it proves to be an evasion more than a decision, since the responsibilities or the qualifications have never been clearly defined. Many cases are cited in which the outsider hired had projected his strengths and camouflaged his shortcomings. Unhappily, the company becomes aware of the compromised selection too late. Damage to the morale of the department has already been done.

Finally, *management often plays games with advancement opportunities*. Word is spread that the opening is there but that the cost of a replacement to fill the position has not been budgeted. "We'll let you know" when the money is available and budgeted for the position, the company says. Or an announcement is made that the company will not fill the position at all but plans to merge it with another position and have the incumbent wear two hats. After a sufficient number of would-be contenders have been discouraged and have made other moves to avoid being dead-ended in their jobs, another announcement follows: the matter has been reconsidered, the merger plan rescinded, and the position will be open after all. Phoney reorganizations are usually an escape route for a company that is inept or indecisive in regard to personnel succession planning. New among the games played is the bottom-line ruse that "we can subcontract the work to the outside," and consequently the position should be liquidated rather than filled. These games are depressants to the competitive climate. The impact upon highly qualified insiders is harsh. Jitters and anxiety pervade the workplace as opportunities are nullified.

These are some of the negative realities in the larger mosaic against which individuals often contend for opportunities and advancement. They take their place alongside other realities that are clearly positive, equitable, and encouraging and conducive to healthy rivalry. Indeed, many companies build a valuable reserve of talent each generation through progressive programs of personnel succession in filling vacancies. They spark advancement opportunities which energize the workplace and have valuable enduring effects on the company's profitability and its stature within the industry. The mature employee has to know that there exists this "mix" of the two. It is foolhardy to ignore these realities. It's difficult enough to strive for the attainable, without living with the deception of the unattainable.

YOUR PERSONAL STRATEGY

In the end you have to confront your own situation and size it up well when planning to compete with a co-worker for advancement. You have to decide whether to compete at all, how to run the race, what attitudes or feelings are best as you compete, and how to handle the likely consequences. People sometimes compete with themselves to enhance their performance, to prove how much they are capable of doing. This is much like the golfer out on the fairway or the putting green who tries to prove that he can play a hole with fewer strokes or improve his way out of a sand trap. It is quite another thing to engage in head-on competition against an opponent. Pressure, fear of failure, excitement, patience, combative instinct, and varied emotions now enter into the picture.

Bear in mind, first, that competing is a relative matter. Much depends on the following six questions:

- Just what is my level of ambition? Where do I want to be in 3–5 years?

- Why am I competing at this stage in my career?
- Against whom?
- What kind of advancement is involved here—in terms of money, prestige, etc.?
- Are the responsibilities and the risks that come with this promotion worth the effort? Do they fit in with my plans?
- What are the likely consequences if I were to pass up this opportunity? if I were to take it on but fail to attain the promotion?

One must answer these fundamental questions before takeoff. Cases abound of employees who are advanced too soon—to responsibilities too large or complex—only to make a rapid descent because they were unable to measure up. Loss of face is not taken lightly. The ignominy is even more severe when envious, resentful colleagues now gleefully gesture at the individual's decline. At other times a person will win the advancement but lose a trusting, valued friend. Histories of erratic job-hopping appear in personnel folders: they often document a career that has been more opportunistic than thoughtful. The lure of more money entices an employee to a better job but one which requires extensive travel. Family life deteriorates because of his absence from home and he has second thoughts as to whether the affluence was worth it all. There is also the scientist who abandoned his field of specialization, crossed functional lines, wants to return, but now finds that he is no longer welcome by his former peers.

These incidents are not cited to present a rationale against competing—not at all. They are mentioned here to indicate why you had better ask those six questions before launching into the competition. You are a better equipped contender when you know the stakes, to what extent you really want to reach for the prize, and why. At that point you are more assured, more self-confident, more tough-minded, and more genuinely competitive.

One can get a remarkable education in career planning these days, so prolific and sound are the many self-help publications and seminars on this subject. But in the long run and for one's personal happiness it is important that purpose (why?) prevail over method (how?) as careers hinge on opportunities and competition.

HEAD-ON COMPETITION

Having made your assessment of the how and the why of competing, assume that your decision is to enter the arena and become a candidate. Now you move from the strategy of personal career planning to *behavioral* considerations— what to do or not to do, when to take certain actions or precautions, with whom to confer, and how to conduct yourself as a serious contender. Proceed on these assumptions:

- The competition will eventually narrow to the three most-promising candidates; you and a peer will be among them.
- All the paperwork, documentation, etc. concerning your credentials and qualifications have been submitted to the appropriate office or selection panel.
- It will be a month or more before the final decision is made as to which candidate will be promoted.

Guides for the Contender

Level with your peer. Tell him that you plan to put in your bid for the position, to compete. Better, indeed, that it come directly from you rather through a third-party source. Otherwise, the communication may become garbled and some distrust introduced.

Empathy, not charity, is due. Put yourself in his shoes and empathize with his ambition and desire to get ahead. He, too, has been waiting for a promising vacancy for some time. But give him nothing that could serve as an advantage or edge. Offer nothing but good will.

Determine how your present boss feels about your candidacy for a job elsewhere in the company. (He is bound to find out sooner or later, so don't alienate him by having him learn about it from another source.) Get a pulse as to whether he will recommend you, block your way, remain neutral. While you do not have to seek his support, it is good to know where he stands. After all, if he resists and will not release you under one pretext or another he can stall long enough to influence the decision adversely.

Focus on your current workload and priorities, since this is the reason for your being on the payroll. Subordinate the ongoing job competition. The decision on the other job may be late in coming, so don't eat up productive time from your present responsibilities.

Do not allow yourself to become vulnerable to the "little" things—recurring lateness, impatience with others, poor listening, absenteeism, humorlessness, excessive time spent in conversation, the just-one-more drink at lunch, missing attendance at a meeting, a delay in submitting the monthly report, or other lapse. Word gets around that you're "slipping" and could hurt your chances in the final hours if the competition is evenly matched.

As unpleasant incidents (rumors, petty arguments) occur during the period of competition, take them in stride. Keep your cool. The unconfirmed rumor will soon evaporate: the misunderstanding will be corrected. If you cannot ignore them, at least, do not pursue them.

If you are going through undue strain or a crisis because of your marriage, health, children, or financial situation, do your best to mask it from 9:00 to 5:00. Release your emotions after the workday. Difficult as it may be you will have to ride out the emotional strain. It's astonishing how well you will recover once you've won the competition and gained the promotion—the counsel of therapists notwithstanding. If you do have one close friend at the office, now is the time when you need his support most and when his trust and confidentiality will really be put to the test.

Do not become involved in any incident that borders on personal misconduct. Any act of real or alleged insubordination, sexual harassment, ethnic or gender discrimination, or violation of a provision in the management/labor agreement can sink your prospects considerably. Very few, if any, co-workers can be counted on to go to your defense. Be very circumspect.

Seize legitimate opportunities to enhance your standing in the race. In fact, do more—create opportunities to give you more credibility as a leading candidate. However, be sure they are bona fide and in the best interests of the department or the company as well as your own.

Learn as much as you can about the vacant job—the functions and responsibilities, priorities, technical aspects, reporting relationships, caliber of staff, and problems. Indeed, probe around (discreetly) to learn all you can as to why the last incumbent left, what were the circumstances; was there undue pressure or a showdown? The information may be valuable "intelligence" in the event that you are called in for interview and dialogue with an officer or the selection panel.

Should you come into useful "inside" information which can reinforce your candidacy, keep it to yourself. If there is no obligation to share it with your rival, then use it to your own advantage.

If you should learn that the particular position is a very sensitive one (such as in legal counsel, research, public relations/speech writing, security, etc.) and you want no part of such sensitive responsibility, reconsider it. You may want to ask that your candidacy be withdrawn. There will be other opportunities.

Trust that your expectations are reasonable. Check out as best as you can that this is not a one-sided race because of your opponent's impressive edge in terms of experience, knowledge, relationships, and proven record of performance. While you may not be a front-runner, at least be assured that you have a fair chance as the final decision nears. Again, you may reconsider staying in contention or pulling out because of certain defeat. You should have made this assessment before, but it is never too late.

No pirating. Be on the alert that your peer should not claim any of *your* work as his own, whether it is a completed delegation, a report, or a special project. Take a firm stand in the event that pirating does occur. Reciprocally, you are not to pirate any of his products.

Exercise discretion about discussing how the competi-

tion is progressing, your feelings, what you plan to do next, or other aspects of the race. Leakage by a secretary, mail clerk, co-worker, contractor, or other person has a way of reaching a wide audience. Play it safe.

Keep preparing yourself for the next higher job, no matter what the outcome in this particular competition. Do it through reading, training seminars, committee or task force assignments, self-improvement aids, more contacts, performance reviews, and other ways. Gain in knowledge, skills, and judgment. The learning process and self-improvement is never ending.

Politicking in the workplace is generally frowned upon, particularly if it is of the usual type. But the desired backing can be accomplished in a quiet, inoffensive way. If you feel that some selected individuals can and would put in a good word for you, send a memo, or take someone out to lunch to influence the selection decision in your behalf, then capitalize on his or her support. Exercise judgment and diplomacy. More important, however, be sure that you know the protocol in the company—how things are done there, what is acceptable behavior.

Finally, and most important to our central theme of good peer relations, *conduct yourself as an upright and moral person.* The rival in this competition is not your enemy; he or she is a rightful adversary.

Guidelines for a Friendly Rival

Refrain from becoming vindictive and insulting under the stress of the competition.

Resist the temptation to "look good" at the expense of the other contender. Don't stoop to snitching to the boss some error which your peer has made, nor neglect to cover his desk so as to deliberately have him fail. If you do, the other members in your department will freeze you as never before and your standing with the boss will also slip badly.

Show maturity as a workplace peer. Do not bad-mouth your rival. It could backfire. Worse—he may someday be your boss.

Injury inflicted on your opponent's reputation is a serious matter and can be brought to litigation. Avoid planting the seed of misinformation and malice about marriage, lifestyle, military record, friendships, financial obligations, or other aspects of his or her personal life. Think about the litigation risk as you make the next mortgage payment.

Visit with him in the office on business-related or other matters, and keep the image of peer respect and acceptance of one another going.

At meetings in which you and your peers are participants, keep the give-and-take professional and courteous. Others are also aware of the rivalry relationship. Don't use the meeting site as a battleground.

Cliques will inevitably do their own thing. Stand aloof from their activities for the present. However, intercede if you can to deter them from smear-campaign or other personal injury tactics.

Continue the usual sociability with your peer, whether it is the bowling team, the weekly luncheon group, or the car-pool ride. Be civil, enjoy the amenities, and put the promotion race on the back burner.

Above all, remain on speaking terms with your rival. The goals and work of your department demand it.

These guidelines are derived from a large fund of experience and practicality. Contending winners and losers, superiors, management consultants, personnel directors, and industrial psychologists have reinforced such observations. Both burning ambition and moral values have their place in the work environment; it's up to you to combine them so that your two priorities—success and good peer relations—can both be met.

AT THE SELECTION INTERVIEW

It is likely that in addition to review of credentials the officer in charge or the selection panel may wish to interview the leading candidates. Sometimes this is referred to as the group oral, where several members direct questions at you and evaluate how you respond. You can be reasonably sure that this is not a random event. They want to gauge your judgment, self-confidence, objectivity, knowledge, attitudes, demeanor, and other factors concerning your readiness.

This interview could be decisive. Give it your very best effort. The following guidelines will be helpful to you:

Talk about work, not people. Focus on systems, processes, production, results, etc. No matter how they try to draw you into discussion about people, keep warding them off in a nice way. Let them make judgments about people if they wish to do so, but don't let yourself fall into this trap.

Be natural. You are not a newcomer; they know you. Just be yourself.

Refrain from repeating your good work and accomplishments. They have already been through your credentials, records of performance, and other documentation. Conserve their time and yours, and refer to your performance only to clarify some point or in direct response to a question.

Avoid cockiness or overconfidence. The promotion isn't in the bag yet.

Avoid being coy. You know you want the job and they know it, too. Shyness may strike one or more members of the panel as affectation.

One or more may try to draw you into discussion about the recent incumbent who left the job and, particularly, about the incidents leading to his departure. Plead innocence. Make the point that you really do not go by mere hearsay. It elevates your reputation for objectivity and good judgment.

They will ask if you feel confident that you can relate to a new role and a changed relationship with your former peers if you should get this promotion. The most acceptable response is: "Yes, I am quite confident. Of course, there is always a transitional period involved in which to make this adjustment—and this will be good for me and for them. We will work this through successfully, I am quite sure." They will regard this as a credible and judicious response.

Address each person as Mr., Miss, Mrs. _____ . If they continue to address you on a first-name basis and feel more comfortable if you were to do the same, then become more informal. Protocol will dictate how you address the company president or vice-president particularly; if in doubt, continue the formal reference to these executives.

Be on time; don't read from written notes; avoid funny

one-liners; don't smoke; and, again, just be natural.

Keep the interview reasonably brief unless they appear to insist on prolonging it. Pick the right cue to make your exit. Remember: the longer the interview the more likely it is that you may misstep, be lured into some argumentative point, or make some silly remark. Try to keep it brief. If they should need more detailed information on some point there is always the telephone.

WHEN THE RACE IS OVER

If you are the winner and get the promotion, you deserve to feel good about it. Celebrate with your family and friends. Psychologically, you need this release, this unwinding. In the office, however, keep the tone modest. Accept congratulations and good wishes graciously. Check with your superiors on the timetable in making the official shift from one position to another, and plan to complete all pending work projects. Make personal visits to thank those who supported or helped you during the recent competition. Have a candid talk with the boss you are about to leave, and let it go on for as long as he desires. This could prove to be a most educational visit as one moves up the ladder. Be sure to take the initiative to drop into the office of your peer and recent adversary, in case he should delay in coming to see you. Exchange a few words and wish him well in his next effort at a promotion. In essence, keep the office behavior modest and proper. Particularly, do not carry a chip on your shoulder and do not plan retaliation against those who supported your rival.

But you may be the loser in this recent race. In this

case your behavior is much more significant. Obviously, you will feel disappointed, perhaps even bitter in defeat, but any display of strong emotion—anger, rashness, tears, open resentment, or outburst—may characterize you as an immature person and the panel may feel it was right in its decision after all. The ability to cope with disappointment is one indicator of emotional stability. Bear this in mind.

In the event that you lose out in the competition, don't sulk, don't blame, don't threaten. These actions are unproductive. Above all, don't disrupt the work of the office or the plant. Some people stew for a long time after a setback such as this; the feeling of being wronged or victimized often takes hold. If you truly feel that the competition was rigged or some other misdeed accounted for the defeat, have a confidential talk with your superior. He may be a very good listener and that in itself may be enough. Or, he may be a person of very good judgment and reason it through with you convincingly that no malice was done. If you still feel there is a strong case to be presented, confer with the personnel director about the right of appeal. He may be as much concerned about the company retaining you as a first-rate employee as about clearing up any skepticism you may have about the recent race. Indeed, he may check thoroughly into matters and advise you about the appeal machinery.

Whatever the aftermath, you now have to exploit all options:

- To try again when another opening occurs;
- To ask for a transfer;

- To adjust to the situation and get on with the job and with a better attitude;
- To leave the company.

In a growing company other opportunities will emerge. It is often best to continue in your present job and to perform well but at the same time be on the alert as to which of the departments is destined to grow and expand in the next several years. At the right time this may be the department to which you would request a transfer.

A FINAL WORD

Stop by to visit your peer, the winner. Wish him well. It's the decent thing to do. Bear in mind that advancement in rank and all that comes with it can be quite hollow unless your working life is a continuing source of genuine satisfaction and self-esteem. And this can hardly ring true unless you are comfortable with your peers and have a strong personal bond with one or more of them.

Chapter 13

How to Cope
with a Setback

When Helen read the terse memo from her superior, "No go; put on shelf," she slumped into the
chair. The humiliation of receiving a curt scribbled
note after all that work was too much to take. Her
thoughts turned to the days and weeks she and Warren had labored over this project. Now it was
brought to a halt; all their combined energies and
abilities down the drain. A bad news call to Warren
was Helen's next move. They met in a nearby diner
for a requiem over a cup of coffee. Her partner refused to put an obituary to the project. He would
lament and groan but refused to go into mourning.
Something could still be done to salvage the sound
proposal, he reasoned, and bring it back to life.

The workplace brings its share of disappointments. Setbacks arise on the job as they do in other arenas of life.
Perhaps this is what partners are for. A healthy co-worker
does not capitulate too easily or too soon; a good team has
the capacity to bounce back in the face of adversity. A
turndown, delay, or other rejection is taken for what it is:
tough luck, but not doom. Convinced of the soundness
and merit of the job done and with evidence to support it,
you and your partner will not throw in the towel. You will

recognize the situation for what it is—a work-performance setback. It could be a setback in regard to an idea proposed, a report, a project, the drafting of a new program, a recommended change, or other substantive proposal beyond the day-to-day work activities. If it's worth submitting, it's worth defending if turned down.

YOUR IDEAS ARE NEEDED

Co-workers, after all, are in the mainstream of work processes and improvements. Since they are close to the operations, they will be expected to have ideas on how work can be accomplished easily, more safely, with fewer errors, or perhaps faster. They are expected to be on the alert to ways in which job performance can be accomplished more economically, more efficiently. Many employees are also expected to be concerned with attaining a more durable company product, enlarging the potential market, improving the office management system, or seeing to it that the company increases its profits. Responsible employees, it is universally agreed, should come forth with their best ideas and special knowledge to help the company attain such gains.

However, the reactions of their superiors to such ideas, proposals, and recommendations cannot be predicted. There is a casualty rate, to be sure. Hindrances, delays, indecision, shelving, or outright rejections often happen. You may encounter grudging reception, part or full acceptance, cautious encouragement, real enthusiasm, or the green light—"let's go." In any case, you give it your best shot.

Partners in the workplace need more than resiliency

and the resolve not to throw in the towel when things go wrong. To deal constructively with a setback they need a combination of:

- A good frame of mind;
- A rigorous, searching analysis of what went wrong, and why;
- A well-conceived effort at recovery by replanning;
- A willingness to mediate and to exercise diplomacy in an effort to get the project back on track.

The most important element of all, however, is the quality of the relationship between the partners faced with adversity. When a team suffers a setback, both partners will need to exhibit humility, good will, resourcefulness, willingness to give of their time and energy to see it through, and mutual reinforcement. The partners must level with each other and be capable of modifying their views and judgments as they go along.

A FRAME OF MIND

Start with *a positive outlook*. Accept reality. Part of the reality is this: "We're at an impasse, yes; we're *not* going to be on a collision course." Whatever might have gone wrong, you're determined to have it corrected. You're still convinced of the soundness of the project, confident that it is worth a try, and intent on persuading your superior to revive it. Your attitude is one of determination not only to salvage the besieged idea but to infuse new life into it as well.

Once you have rallied a bit, *keep up the momentum*. An

unexpected piece of good luck, a "break," may accelerate things even more. Counteract any remaining doubts you or your partner may still have. Ward off any cockiness, rigidity, or inflated ego. It is quite possible that what has gone wrong might be due to a deficiency on your part.

Avoid any tendency to blame yourself, your partner, or others. *Don't seek a scapegoat.* Finding blame is fruitless; finding a solution is productive. Concentrate on maintaining your reputation for performance capability and your standing in the department and among your peers.

Show no overconcern about having been clipped. Keep as busy as possible at productive tasks and responsibilities. You do not need a chaplain on whom to unload any distress. Meaningful, productive work is adequately therapeutic. Some self-examination may be helpful, of course, but don't overdo it.

Very important to your frame of mind is the need to *shut off certain hurtful reactions and temptations.* The impulse to become angry at the boss (or whoever was responsible for the turndown) is understandable. Under such emotional stress, anger could lead to an outburst of words you will later regret. Don't fall into the anger trap; it is counterproductive. Avoid any semblance of *apathy.* An attitude of indifference to your job, particularly because of this particular incident of a setback, will be observed by those around you. Snide remarks or rumors are then likely to make the grapevine. Your attitude should not reflect mental fatigue or emotional strain even if you do experience these.

There is usually nothing ominous in a one-case rejection or turndown. Consequently, *do not read signs of threat into the incident* or predict unfortunate events yet to come. Unless you've been in the doghouse and this is merely another in a series of turndowns, there is no reason to suspect that hard times are ahead. Clearly, there is to be no sense of failure, no ashes and sackcloth, no self-imposed isolation. Show neither frustration nor bafflement. Mature employees are not thrown easily.

Your healthy frame of mind is the springboard from which to take off. If you follow some of the above guidelines, the prospects are greatly improved for moving toward a constructive course of action.

SEARCH FOR WHAT WENT WRONG

Any number of factors could account for the setback: your approach, communications, people, the method, the presentation, timing, the boss's behavior, or the handling of the project as a whole. As you search for the cause:

- Ask the right questions and probe the vulnerable areas;
- Accept the findings objectively, and distinguish between hard facts and surface opinions—and be sure to verify and confirm;
- Assess the truly relevant and important findings that finally emerge, and evaluate what impact these findings might have had on the outcome of the project.

Do not flinch, cover up, or alibi away any unpleasant findings even if they hurt your ego. For a better understanding of what went wrong you might ask questions such as these:

- Did we move too fast; were we too aggressive? Would the results have been different if we had changed the pace?
- Was the timing right for this kind of project, in priority and reception? If not, why was the timing off?
- Were one or two key officials overlooked in our contacts and communication? Were they miffed?
- Were any deadlines missed? If so, were they really consequential?
- Were the back-up data—statistics, charts, illustrations, etc.—unconvincing? What would have made them more convincing?
- To what extent did we hit a sensitive nerve—flouted tradition, insulted a sacred cow in the organization, stepped on someone's toes? Could this have been averted?
- Was the entire project possibly too ambitious, too cumbersome an undertaking? Should it have been cut down to size?
- Did we take so low-key an approach as to possibly lessen our project's importance as a priority matter?
- How clear was the purpose or goal? Should we have asked for more clarification at the very outset?
- Did we keep our superior posted regularly as the project progressed? If not frequently enough, why?
- How extensive and useful was the feedback received as we moved from one stage to the next?
- Did we utilize all available information? If not, what important information was still missing?
- Were internal politics in any way an impediment? How do we know?
- Did we deal with the wrong level(s) of management? Or, did we omit certain staff offices which could have helped us?

- Did we present too many recommendations? Too few?
- As to the final presentation (written or oral), could this have been more persuasive? How?

The answers to this wide range of questions should finally bring us to the point of asking these three crucial and summary questions: (1) What have we learned from this experience? (2) Which factors could have converted possible failure into success? (3) Can the project still be salvaged? If it can, what options are open in trying to revive it?

Finally, you have to contend with some *unknown* about the boss and his terse memo, "No go; put on shelf." If he is uncertain, hedging, his answer may be an act of indecision rather than a definite negative. Or, he might be under considerable pressure in dealing with other matters in the in-basket. Confronted with a number of things on his desk, he might be conveying the point that this particular item no longer rates a high priority, so it is relegated to "the shelf." Bosses are also known to go by whim and fancy now and then. Some would argue, perhaps, that that is their prerogative. Your boss exercises his authority, without explanation, to ignore the completed report. Wasteful, to be sure, but it does occur. And, there is this last big unknown: the boss does not like the completed project recommendations and rejects them, but doesn't have the backbone to level with his subordinates. This lack of candor leaves them stranded. In essence, even with the most rigorous search for answers, you are still left with the mystery of human behavior. The behavior of the

boss defies the search and leaves you, at least for the pres--
ent, with a number of unknowns.

RECOVERY—REPLAN AND ACTION

The first step toward recovery is acknowledgment. With
the analysis results before you, acknowledge the deficien-
cies or weaknesses, the marginal features, and the strong
points in the handling and completion of the project. At
this point the boss may be willing to "open up" and cite
his own criticisms, good and bad. This would of course be
welcome, since the important goal is to keep the project
alive, take it off the shelf.

You and your partner would do well, after the analysis,
to prepare a list of options or an action chart. In this way
you will be prepared for your next meeting with the boss.

Possible Options and Actions toward Recovery

☐ Re-examine the documents and file to check on hand-
written comments, attached memos, revised drafts,
etc., for possible clues.

☐ Find out where the sources of opposition or resistance
might be, then confer with key people to straighten
out misunderstandings.

☐ Determine clearly what each partner will do.

☐ Build in more information or new information as may
be needed.

☐ Rewrite the report in a more fitting style—possibly
briefer, less academic, clearer, less dogmatic.

☐ Get more cooperation, and possibly backing, from other departments.

☐ Counteract the rumors, if at all possible.

☐ Acknowledge weak points, gaps, and other marginal features of the report.

☐ Capitalize on better timing, for greater prospect of acceptance next time.

☐ Animate the report, perhaps, with more graphics.

☐ Simplify the project, make it less cumbersome.

☐ Get new feedback from different sources.

☐ Meet with the superior, informally.

☐ Tap the views of staff specialists who were overlooked before.

☐ Build in more and possibly better controls.

☐ "Draw out" the boss for his candid criticism, good and bad.

☐ Build on what has been learned from the search and analysis.

☐ Take advantage of related committee reports or other supportive work.

Three commitments bind you and your partner throughout the process: to show mutual support and reinforce each other; to get the project off the shelf and to keep it alive; and, to exercise all persuasion for the chance to rework it.

At the actual meeting with the boss, follow through by emphasizing your awareness of the potential use of the project and your concern for its success. Make the point that to keep it on the shelf or otherwise dispose of it would deprive the departments and the company of a much-needed improvement. Let him know that after nosing around, during the search, you probably know considerably more than has been said, understand the opposition and the doubts that arose, and have since conferred with some of the people and put straight some of the misunderstandings.

Emphasize your strong desire to rework the report so that it will be better and more acceptable. Stress the element of practicality; how practical and functional the findings and recommendations will be to those concerned. Hammer away at this point. If he has further doubts, give him a body of evidence—facts, examples, experiences, confirmation. If the boss is still wavering, argue in behalf of at least giving it a trial run on an experimental basis and then to judge the results and gains at the close of a given period. Be persuasive, and hope you will be given the "green light" to rework it.

The kind of discussion you should aim for in this meeting is one concerned with exchanging views, comparing notes, bringing the boss up to date, matching sets of facts, etc. It is *not* confrontation, in the sense of trying to resolve a conflict.

RIGHT APPROACH

The approach you take in preparing for this meeting and in handling it can make or break the total effort to bounce back. Tact, discretion, sensitivity, and manner enter into the right approach. Call it diplomacy, if you will; the point is to avoid alienation and to meet and confer with mutual concern. As long as you are on speaking terms and there is some existing good will, you have a good chance of winning the case to salvage and rework the project. As you go forward with your salvage plans, observe these guidelines:

- Stay within the chain of command. Give your boss no cause for personal or official embarrassment by going around him or over his head.
- Do not violate any confidential information.
- Try to meet with him at a time when the pressure is off and he is more relaxed, and especially a time when there will be very few interruptions.
- Avoid an all-or-nothing situation that could place you and your boss in a polarized position. Leave room for flexibility, bending, or adaptation.
- In a friendly but sober manner air any misunderstandings which seem to exist. Adjust the differences as the talk progresses.
- Expect to gain some points and to yield on other points.
- Not all questions need to be resolved at one sitting; some may be handled later.
- Do not bad-mouth others.
- Do not bluff. You may be taken up on it and possibly lose your credibility.
- Watch your words; they often betray emotions. Avoid words that suggest distrust, bitterness, or questioned loyalty; nevertheless, be candid about the issue, the impact, and the need for constructive action.
- You may not need an intermediary, but if a key official (and one respected by your boss and by you) should want to intervene and speak in behalf of the project, do not turn down the offer.

In summary, "bouncing back" is more than just a matter of mutual concern and moral courage among partners;

it is a *process* by which individual moral courage, the proper frame of mind, hard work to uncover what went wrong, a well-planned effort to recover, and a good approach to dialogue with the boss all combine to make your success possible.

WHEN IT'S ALL OVER

It's never easy to hear that adversity and setbacks are "good for you," but it's often true, whether it's a mixed project or a soured relationship with a work partner. Your project could go down the tube despite your best efforts, or you and your teammate could find that you just don't work well together, or that there is some personal incompatibility. If that is the case, it's probably better not to pursue the project or to try to work together over the long haul. But let's assume that the two of you feel a certain amount of good will toward one another and enjoy the prospect of continuing to be partners.

Now is a good time to take the next step in your friendship. Perhaps you'd like to mark the occasion now that the meeting with the boss—which you planned for so carefully—is finally over. Celebrate together, be more open, talk about more personal matters (put aside the project for a while). There is no time like the present for strengthening this friendship. You have been through a great deal together.

Chapter 14

Disagreement, Criticism, and Aggravation— You Can Handle Them All

In a healthy organization people talk back. They do not do so in order to be defiant, abrasive, or negative, nor is there an attempt at deliberate sabotage. Democracy in the workplace entitles us to dissent when we are moved to do so. Just as we widen the door of communication to permit people to express their opinions, so we recognize dissent as another form of expression. Honest dissent is for the most part an expression of conscience. People stand up for what they believe in—their convictions, values, judgments, and viewpoints—and hope that their peers will do the same. The two views will at times fail to mesh; they may even be in direct opposition. Disagreement often ensues. At some point the disagreement will have to be settled, so that the two workers, the department, or the company can get on with the show.

People disagree and in some instances quarrel at length because of their different ways of perceiving things. The journalists Woodward and Armstrong revealed in *The Brethren* that even the dignified justices of the lofty Supreme Court of the United States have their disagreements. Despite their robes and the responsibilities on their shoulders, they have their squabbles. Historians tell us that beneath Gilbert and Sullivan's enormously popular collaboration were "two hearts that beat as two." Gilbert and Sullivan did not get along at all and had many disagreements, but in spite of their differences they managed to collaborate effectively for fifteen years and to produce real gems of light opera.

In today's business world we read now and then of a vice-president leaving the company for reasons of difference of philosophy or disagreement about new plans. Employees customarily air differences and disagreements in staff meetings. We are obligated professionally and morally as working men and women to deal with our differences, and we'll get along far better if we can deal with them openly, honestly, and with a modicum of grace. A good place to begin is to develop an awareness of how these disagreements arise.

THE CAUSES OF DISAGREEMENT

Disagreement is attributed to a variety of causes. Misjudging a statement is one basic cause. Poor listening is another. Stress, induced by personal circumstances that carry over into the workplace, is recognized as a prevalent reason for nervousness that in turn can provoke disagreement with others. Researchers cite loneliness as a serious cause of disaffection, particularly among "singles" who are lonely because of the death of a spouse or the unhappy dissolution of a marriage. Loneliness produces anxiety or anger, and those feelings are difficult for people to hide as they go about their workplace duties.

Just plain inability to see eye-to-eye with a peer can engender disagreement. Dissatisfaction with working conditions will sometimes manifest itself in opposition to just about anything or anyone around. Failure to be credited with a job well done may evoke bitterness and disagreeableness as a form of personal protest. A person's vantage point in the organization could well lead to disagreement because of a difference in perspective—i.e., you are at headquarters and your peer is in the field; you are in a staff position and he or she in a position of line responsibility; you have a legal counsel function and your peer works in the Personnel Department. A keen observer of corporate bureaucracy coined this motto: "How you stand on an issue depends on where you sit." Differences in rank or pay can also induce attitudes that lead to disagreement.

Personal characteristics and flaws must surely be counted among the causes of chronic disagreement. Most workplaces have their share of argumentative and quarrelsome people. Arrogance is no stranger to the workplace, either. Also in our midst are a few people so acerbic that they seem incapable of a moment's good cheer. Pettiness abounds and contributes to disagreement. Co-workers are known to retreat under the bureaucratic umbrella with these cliches: "That's not my job" . . . "I can't spare the time to clear it up" . . . "We just didn't hit it off at the meeting" . . . "Nobody did it for me, so why should I now be the nice guy" . . . "It wasn't my idea in the first place" . . . "You can check the manual"—and other expressions of unwillingness to be agreeable.

How do we cope with all this conflict?

HOW TO PROCEED

The primary goal is to *keep disagreement at a minimum* and to handle it well when it arises. Begin with objectives and aims. Your company is probably in an industry where competitors are out to beat each other to the greater share of the market. Sales, innovations, profits, and growth are the dominant considerations. Employees are on the payroll to enable the company to achieve these to the optimum while complying with government regulations. Company thinking is dominated, as it should be, by objectives, goals, strategies, plans, and resources. These govern all else in the organization. Make it your immediate goal *to help others recognize that the job comes first, the personal considerations second*. Often, if one's attention is really on the job, potential disagreements will disperse before they become a real problem. It is understandable that within the complex of your organization there will emerge various ideas, views, and proposals. All will not be compatible. Differences and disagreements will be voiced. But if the main objective is to get the job done, the disagreements may naturally fall by the wayside.

Recognize the sensitive areas which tend to generate most of the disagreements. Among the thorny issues are priorities, budgets, standards, staffing, authority/responsibility status, and decision-making prerogative. Expertise in itself takes a back seat for a while. Each employee believes that he or she deserves more resources; each argues on behalf of professionalism as he or she sees it. Changes can be particularly galling; change often generates resistance. People fear that their status or security may be threatened and their departmental functions and stability challenged. Emotions ride high as changes are proposed. Yet change is the lifeblood of an organization. Be sensitive and alert to these thorny issues and do advance planning to handle them better, whether you're the boss, a middle manager, or a newcomer in an entry-level position.

Scout the troublemakers, those who arouse disagreement or who are intent upon blocking agreement. Know their motives and means. If their activities materially affect the progress of the department in moving toward objectives and goals, the supervisor or manager in charge should know about it. It may come to a showdown, but it will be a showdown between the rebel and the supervisor. In short, if the disagreement cannot be resolved personally between you and a disagreeable peer, it will have to be resolved officially in the chain of command. Exercise discretion so that you do not alienate the other person.

Don't step in too quickly. Co-workers who disagree on some aspect of their work can usually accommodate and adapt to bring about a workable solution on their own. Peers manage to find clues, get to the bottom of the problem, and work out a means of clearing up the disagreement. They are quite capable of disentangling the strands. Give them enough leverage to arrive at the best solution.

When you do have to intervene or when you become involved in a disagreement with a peer, keep in mind that in dealing with any disagreement you should handle the matter in stages or in some sequence. It may help to follow these ten steps:

Disagreement, Criticism, and Aggravation

1. Begin with intervention: take the initiative to determine what seems to have gone wrong and how it can be set right. Don't let much time elapse.
2. Assess your peer's feelings and try to allay the hurt feelings he has because of the misunderstanding.
3. Talk things over with your co-worker and stress your desire to (a) define and articulate the issue more sharply so that it is fully clarified; (b) unfreeze any resolute stand which you or he may hold, and (c) agree to reopen the discussion and proceed on another plane. Dogmatism and rigidity are severe barriers; with tact and prudence they can be removed through dialogue.
4. Produce as much *objective* evidence or proof as you can to support your own viewpoint. At this point facts must displace opinions. The evidence may be more effective than your own pitch.
5. Educate one another so that there is reciprocal understanding of each other's perception of the issue, the technical content, and the state of the art in the particular discipline involved. Educate each other, too, to the pros and cons so that the problem can be seen from both sides.
6. Expect some degree of bend or compromise on your own part and his. Have an open mind to the soundness of some compromise.
7. Encourage one another and share the optimism that the final agreement will prove to be all to the good. Thinking so may well make it so.
8. Try to carry on the exchange or dialogue privately. Avoid any public display. Only when absolutely necessary should you involve others, such as the supervisor, another peer, or a staff specialist.

9. If agreement is to be formalized (adjudicating the disagreement) record the new agreement so that there is a written document of what was agreed to, by whom, when, and with what conditions. All parties concerned should have a copy.
10. Always level with your co-worker. Trying to evade a disagreement or submerge it is unproductive.

Among peers of good will, the overriding concern should be mutuality. In a truly integrative resolution, the *main* concerns and motives of each person are attained. Not all, perhaps, but the main ones. The outcome then becomes one of win/win, not win/lose. The differences that do remain are the less consequential ones that can be readily adjusted.

Again, bitter medicine can often cure, and a disagreement can sometimes serve to strengthen and solidify a peer friendship. When the negotiations are finished and the disagreement resolved, it may be time for you and your peer to move onto a more personal level of friendship. Have a meal together, or go somewhere where you can be open and informal and can focus on the event from a *personal*, rather than a professional, standpoint. Now is a time to celebrate a job well done—a conflict resolved. For the moment, you are in accord, and your friendship can flourish. Who knows—perhaps next week another conflict may arise—or one or the other of you may have to face another difficult situation: the need to give or take criticism.

GIVING OR TAKING CRITICISM

Since co-workers differ and disagree at times in regard to their respective beliefs, values, ideas, or viewpoints, there are bound to be incidents in which one will be critical of the other. The criticism may not be malicious or harsh but it will still be jarring. After all, criticism is derived from someone else's value system or judgment of how you should have perceived a problem and acted upon it. Subjectivity always enters into such a judgment.

Nevertheless, assessment or evaluation is essential if we are to understand one another and especially if our discussion of the disagreement is to be at all fruitful. Well-intended and constructive criticism is in itself an act of friendship between peers in that it serves the well-being of the co-worker. Failure to criticize for fear of hurting the other person is failure to help your work friend grow. Feedback, both positive and negative, serves a useful purpose. It opens one's eyes to weaknesses as well as strengths, to other options and possibilities. Improvement in personal behavior and in joint performance can hardly be attained without candid feedback. In many instances the feedback is not critical at all. Indeed, it may be reassuring and encouraging and may serve to reinforce what he has done well.

But giving or receiving constructive criticism is not always a pleasurable venture. In many instances, the other person may not be able to take it. Criticism is rarely taken kindly. Fragile egos are easily damaged and defensiveness almost always follows. The receiver will often deny, defend, alibi, or counteract under the stress of an injured ego. Few people are ready to acknowledge a weakness or an error in judgment. To do so is deflating and involves a loss of self-esteem. People become particularly agitated when the criticism reflects upon their long-held values and beliefs—more so than when their knowledge or skills are called into question.

The source of the criticism makes a difference, too. Whether it comes from an older or a younger person, a member of the same or opposite sex, an acknowledged expert in the field or an ordinary practitioner, a seasoned manager or a newly designated supervisor, can make a big difference in how the criticism is received and with what degree of emotional upset.

Much has been written about the place of criticism between boss and subordinate. Bosses criticize fairly or unfairly in regard to the performance of their subordinates. Some are overcritical; others are fatherly or motherly and do not offer enough criticism. Some employees view their boss's criticism as an act of personal dislike, while others contend that they have to take too much of it. All criticism and no praise is the lament of many subordinates.

Our main concern, here, is not with criticism that is based on organizational hierarchy, appraisal of performance, reward and punishment, and the need for rational control within a company. Our real concern is with peer criticism and how to blend it into a good working relationship with a co-worker.

SOME GUIDELINES

Bear in mind the premise that peer standing means just that—parity. This makes the one-to-one relationship and mutual criticism that much more sensitive, and requires more alertness to several concerns: Always remember that it may be presumptuous for one of similar standing or rank to pass judgment on the other. Remember, too, that you are expressing only a personal opinion; the criticism may or may not be warranted. Finally, always bear in mind that criticizing your peer may damage the existing relationship and make the task of working together more difficult in the future. These guidelines may be helpful to you either in giving or taking criticism:

- Get the facts straight so as to confirm that the criticism is warranted.
- Criticize the act, not the person. Pointing up the question, "What caused us to delay in trying the new experimental approach?" is likely to be far less a blow than the direct statement, "You should have had more sense than to continue on with the old project."
- Criticize your work friend privately. Make sure that you are not being overheard.
- First empathize, then criticize. Your colleague may be inclined then to restate his viewpoint differently or less rigidly.
- Keep your comments at an intellectual, substantive level, not an emotional one.
- Focus on the positive side of the problem, particularly on how things can still be corrected.
- Recognize that it is unwise to press him to admit a mistake or an error. Keep the substantive discussion going and as it evolves he may eventually come to the point of acknowledging that perhaps he could have made a better judgment. Accept the admission quietly, without comment.

- Be specific about what can be done to erase the disagreement. Generalities are of little use here; get down to specifics about the next constructive step to take.
- The word "we" engenders more enthusiasm and willingness to act than repeated use of the words "you" or "I." Disagreement and removal of that disagreement involves two parties; keep it in that spirit even if you know quite well that one is less culpable than the other.
- Concentrate on solution, not on fixing blame.
- Keep building on your peer's strengths and self-esteem. Self-confidence spurs corrective action.
- Watch your tongue. No snide remarks, no bad-mouthing, no accusations. Failing to keep civility can deal a severe blow to your relationship.

Two final observations are worth bearing in mind. A mixture of praise and criticism does more for the peer relationship and correction of disagreement than does criticism alone. Use the "mix" judiciously. Every person being criticized fears loss of face. Help your peer avoid any sense of humiliation. The art of handling disagreement agreeably is a learnable art. You are quite capable of mastering it.

THOSE IRRITATING MANNERISMS

We deal with imperfections wherever we encounter them. Your office friend's shortcomings are part of the imperfect workplace. They can be particularly annoying to you, because of the close proximity of one desk or work table to another. You feel captive. Cramped quarters in the work space, locker room, meeting room, computer site, or other location add to the dilemma. Under such conditions your officemate's irritating habits or manners can be very vexing.

Scan this list of habits or mannerisms that at times are offensive to one's sensibilities:

- excessive cologne or perfume
- telling off-color jokes
- clock-watching
- finger-snapping
- banging the typewriter
- adding more photos and mementos to the wall
- bumming cigarettes, candy, cookies
- poor grammar
- sloppy clothes
- loud telephone voice
- stretching feet on the top of desk
- belching
- carrying the flu or other virus to the office
- scanty attire
- conducting personal business on the phone
- frequent talk of union business
- singing, humming, whistling
- ethnic slurs
- gossiping
- crabbing about conditions
- stream of visitors to socialize
- yawning
- poor posture
- shifting chairs noisily
- playing the radio
- long-winded stories
- constant coughing, rasping
- making arrangements for still another business trip
- window-opening, window-closing
- yacking—family, TV programs, etc.

BEGIN WITH UNDERSTANDING

While there is no specific prescription to cure your co-worker's bad habits, you can ameliorate the situation by

taking the right approach. Try these five steps—or which-
ever of them will work for you.

1. Sort out in your own mind how these mannerisms affect you. If they strike you as crude or tactless, you
   have a right to be annoyed. Putting up with aggrava-
   tion for part of the eight-hour day can be irksome. Do
   someone's mannerisms actually affect the quality of
   your work? At times they can, and do, interfere with
   concentration, clear thinking, energy level, timing, or
   output.

2. Recognize that although you and your colleague are
   work partners, there may be quite a difference in
   your backgrounds. Tact, refinement, and taste may
   have been emphasized in your upbringing while your
   office mate may have had quite another kind of exposure and may be lacking in propriety and decorum.
   Perhaps he doesn't know the difference between
   proper and improper office conduct or is unmindful of
   its effect on others. Try to understand.

3. Learn to tolerate eccentricity. None of us has a mo-
   nopoly on peculiarity. Whether it be a high-pitched
   voice, combing one's hair every half hour, scraping
   fingernails against the paper, addressing everyone as
   "pal" or "dearie," snubbing anyone who dares to
   brown-bag at lunch, or any other oddity—each of us
   has some whim or idiosyncrasy that we may un-
   knowingly inflict upon others. This in itself does not
   label one as a nut, but a combination of weird habits
   adds up to an oddball.

   Eccentrics have their place in the business world as
   long as they continue to earn their way on the company payroll. Tolerance of their ways is the best strategy.

4. Consider the motives for behavior. A work partner can be mean-spirited for one reason or another. In his resentment he is determined to make the workday uncomfortable for everyone—and perhaps particularly for you. This is his way of expressing his hostility but in a covert manner so as not to invite a clash. Indeed, the resentment may not even be directed toward you; it may be at the company, and you are simply a convenient target. Remember that not all habits or mannerisms are due to physiology or lack of decorum and etiquette; some are psychological devices.

5. Let's come right out with it and acknowledge that some of our co-workers are downright crude and nasty. They are disdainful of anything proper and discreet. Such co-workers, few as they are in the workplace, do not make good partners in the office, plant, factory, store, warehouse, station, or other work site. What do we do when one of these lemons sits across the room from us for most of our waking hours?

APPROACHES

Do not expect miracles. Recognize that in trying to get relief from such irritating conduct you are unlikely to achieve an all-or-nothing result. You can, however, realistically expect your co-workers to *reduce* or curb the extent or frequency of the annoyance. But you will have to be patient, tactful, and circumspect.

Constructive ways of dealing with irritating habits and mannerisms include both direct and indirect approaches. Try the direct approaches first.

Trigger his awareness. Maybe he did not realize that

his habit annoyed people; nobody had brought it to his attention before. A basically fair and considerate person will make a special effort to curb an irritating habit once he knows it is bothersome to others.

Try an occasional good-natured dig. It need not be a caustic remark. Just a repeated twit or jibe at the right time, and perhaps with the right humor, might make him more conscious of the fact that his whistling or endless throat clearing is driving you up the wall.

Cajole him with "I enjoy working with you, Phil, but . . ." and then indicate how you would enjoy the workday more if he would move his chair less often and less noisily or quit the singing and whistling.

Talk straight and firmly when telling someone that you are offended by off-color jokes or racist slurs. Make it clear that you are not a party to either. Tell him that these are offensive to you—and to most others as well.

Contribute to his social education if you are able to do it subtly and graciously. It is never too late to learn and he may appreciate knowing what is proper and acceptable. He may even remove his feet from the top of the desk or subdue that boisterous laughter on the telephone.

If you have alerted him before, then repeat as necessary. He will come to know that you mean it. Stand firm with "I've mentioned this several times before, Henry. I can't concentrate on my work with all this noise. Please, once again, cut down the loudness and laughter."

If these direct approaches don't work, or if you are reluctant to be so up-front, use a more indirect approach:

Select a third party—someone who is friendly with and respected by your officemate. Explain the situation and ask if he would be willing to intervene and persuade the offender to curb the irritating habit.

The "silent treatment" is always an option. If the offender should be puzzled and ask what is wrong, you can then express candidly the extent to which his habit has affected you or your work. Indicate that you've tried to bring it to his attention before and that your patience has worn thin. In the interest of preserving a more amicable relationship within the office he may take the matter more seriously.

Should the annoyance seriously affect your work over a long period of time, you may have to *discuss it confidentially with your boss.* Give him the whole background of how it affects your productivity, what efforts you have made to talk it over, and elicit his suggestions about how to improve the situation. Avoid asking for relocation to another office, a private phone to which you can have ready access, a transfer, a ban on the frequent social visitors, or other action. Let *him* consider the possible actions after mulling over the situation. He will probably take some action because of the impact on the productivity of his department. The means for doing it will vary from one supervisor to another. Most supervisors will make an effort to solve the problem amicably and quietly so as to avoid making a "big deal" of it.

WHEN THERE'S NO WAY OUT

What if your strategies, direct and indirect, fail to work and the boss doesn't take your distress seriously? Perhaps you really are too thin-skinned or touchy about office hygiene and etiquette. If that is so, you will have to bend and compromise. This may be in the best interests of the department as a whole.

Don't threaten to quit or give an ultimatum; bite the bullet. Try to use this situation as a chance to practice tolerance, understanding, and patience. Slowly, gradually, and with humor, go back to those five steps and try them again. You may be surprised to find that they will eventually work and that your co-worker may even become a friend.

Perhaps the most significant point is this: there is generally no justification for having incidents of annoyance erupt into a severe personality clash between office co-workers, nor need work productivity be impaired. Create awareness, show the other party how his habit offends you personally, try both direct and indirect approaches, and involve the boss only when other measures have failed. Be optimistic: trust that the annoyance will be reduced or curbed. If the irritant goes away completely, consider that a bonus.

One of the lessons learned in the workplace is the capacity for tolerance. We tolerate working conditions, poor supervision, unjust policies, and inadequate means of recognition. We tolerate disagreement and criticism. Add to these the need to tolerate some of the whims and odd mannerisms of your co-worker. Try to elevate your tolerance level while, at the same time, you try to improve *his* office etiquette.

Although some people seem to be impervious to disapproval, criticism, suggestion, even overt pleas for a change in behavior, they are, under the tough skin, "taking it all in." Eventually, it will probably penetrate. As a member of your workplace group, you are constantly observing and being observed. Use this as an opportunity to help others overcome weaknesses and foibles, to strengthen their good qualities, to become better working partners and friends.

Chapter 15

Socializing and Sex – The Sensitive Areas

In one of the most comprehensive surveys on the subject of friendship, a series of questions dealt with the activities that friends engaged in most frequently. *Talking* proved to be the number one activity. Interviews with men and women confirmed the fact that talk ranges from mundane chats about clothing and cars to philosophical discussions on the meaning of life. *Doing*—helping out on some matter, sharing a sport or activity, going somewhere—is a runner-up. *Talking* and *doing* are the dominant activities.

ALL FRIENDSHIPS NEED BOUNDARIES

In your own experience you have probably encountered some of the sensitive areas, perhaps warily, within the wide range of activities among friends. These need to be observed if you are to keep any friendship healthy. Within a workplace setting, people are in close contact with each other for eight hours of the day, but too much intimacy can be suffocating. Move slowly, and don't allow a friendship to escalate to the point where you become uncomfortable with it. A good way to avoid this is to stop short of any activity that might take the friendship farther than you want it to go.

HOW FAR IS TOO FAR?

People do a number of things together in socializing as work friends: shopping, watching a sports event, going to a movie, eating out, playing tennis, attending a meeting or a lecture, taking their children together to a museum or a show. There is little likelihood of problems arising in such types of get-together, although some people may wish to limit their friendships to less personal activities.

In this chapter we will outline and discuss those areas of socialization that can be, and often are, sensitive ones. But first, take this questionnaire in order to assess your *current position* vis-à-vis work friendship and your present attitude toward the various activities those friendships involve. Be candid.

YOUR WORKPLACE SOCIABILITY PROFILE

PERSONAL/SOCIAL ACTIVITY TOGETHER

I have done this with *one* work friend, possibly two, within the past year (enter X mark in the correct blank):

	Never	Rarely	Occasionally	Often
Exchange birthday greetings or gifts	☐	☐	☐	☐
Exchange article from newspaper/magazine	☐	☐	☐	☐
Share anecdotes, jokes, memories	☐	☐	☐	☐
Borrow a book	☐	☐	☐	☐
Confide, share a secret	☐	☐	☐	☐

Have a personal, perhaps intimate, talk	☐	☐	☐	☐
Discuss religious background and beliefs	☐	☐	☐	☐
Share a new, or innovative, idea	☐	☐	☐	☐
Criticize each other, constructively	☐	☐	☐	☐
Help improve each other's habits, dress, mannerisms, etc.	☐	☐	☐	☐
Discuss personal ambitions, career plans, job opportunities	☐	☐	☐	☐
Compete in a sport	☐	☐	☐	☐
Attend a religious service	☐	☐	☐	☐
Attend a sports event	☐	☐	☐	☐
Go shopping	☐	☐	☐	☐
Give a reference in behalf of his/her child	☐	☐	☐	☐
Attend a movie, concert, play, or museum event	☐	☐	☐	☐
Visit at his or her home	☐	☐	☐	☐
Have a drink during off-work hours	☐	☐	☐	☐
Telephone him or her at home	☐	☐	☐	☐

Borrow or lend money	☐	☐	☐	☐
Dine at a restaurant	☐	☐	☐	☐
Meet his or her spouse and socialize	☐	☐	☐	☐
Go to a party	☐	☐	☐	☐
Participate in a community program	☐	☐	☐	☐

YOUR PROFILE

If your responses appear largely in the *"Never"* or *"Rarely"* columns, you have a *LOW* work-friendship sociability level.

If they are largely in the *"Occasionally"* column, with some spill-over into the *"Rarely"* or *"Often"* columns, you have a *MODERATE* work-friendship sociability level.

If your responses are mainly in the *"Often"* and *"Occasionally"* columns, your work-friendship sociability level is *HIGH*.

Your "Low," "Moderate," or "High" score on the questionnaire does not type you as a poor, average, or good friend: it merely indicates present sociability. You will want to be aware of the sensitive areas even if you are not encountering them today. Things change; and, too, awareness can be helpful in counseling friends and others who may be encountering more touchy situations than you are.

BEING ALERT TO THE SENSITIVE AREAS

Dining

Chances are that you enjoy sharing a meal with your work friend. Having lunch together presents a good opportunity for conversation. However, avoid making a ritual of eating with the same co-worker each day. Others may soon write you off as a lunch partner because of your un-availability. Vary your lunch and coffee-break compan-ions. A good mixer gains exposure to new happenings within the company. Both you and your work friend will have more and fresher news items to bring to the table if you each have lunch with many other people. More im-portant, avoid feeding the grapevine the notion that this twosome must have something secretive going in their lunchtime tête-à-tête. An occasional breakfast or dinner together is fine; but if you are seen together at those meals frequently, tongues will wag.

Drinking

Many people perceive a regular drinking pair as too inti-mate. It's relaxing and pleasurable to have a drink with a friend at the close of the day, but do it in moderation. Know your capacity for holding liquor. Be aware that too many drinks poses a problem of how to get home safely. If faced with the choice, take a taxicab or a bus rather than have the work friend drive you to your home. Drinking plus being escorted home only feeds the rumor-mongers. Drink together occasionally to relax and talk, or to cele-brate an event, but vary the company; ask others to join in and make it a group table. Be concerned about your repu-tation.

Discussing Salaries

The curiosity to find out who earns how much money is always a temptation in the workplace. If the answer simply ended there, the curiosity would be satisfied. But implications are drawn and then other questions and problems ensue: How come she earns so much more than I? Is it fair to give a relative newcomer a salary almost equal to mine after I've been here three years? If we both have the same title, Senior Clerk, why should there be a variation in our salaries? Relationships can become touchy because wrong implications are drawn from the answers. In most cases the facts are distorted, and so there remains the feeling that salary equity or fair treatment has been breached.

The fault often lies largely in lack of understanding of a company's personnel policies. As employees we need to understand what constitutes the job evaluation and compensation system within our company. Not all people come in at the same entry-level salary; some are given more credit for prior experience and education. Many raises and salary progressions are based on merit and not on equity. Some supervisors are more prone to recommend salary increments for their employees, while others are negligent or indifferent. Fringe benefits, "perks," special rates, incentive pay, and other factors beyond base pay can influence the compensation package. Job responsibilities change and become more complex, although position titles may remain unchanged. Some employees choose certain benefits to complement those of a spouse working elsewhere to achieve a more well-rounded yield of health insurance benefits, and they forego others. Salary surveys are updated for some departments and woefully outdated for others. The union representing clerical workers in the company may have won notable gains for its members while the union representing the technical employees has been unassertive and made only minimal salary increases for its people.

When you have a better grasp of the variables that influence salary differences you will understand that this is largely a management-employee policy rather than a peer-to-peer matter. Although many companies have personnel rules to guard against leakage of information about salaries, the guessing game still goes on among co-workers as to who earns what.

If you have reason to feel unfairly treated and wronged in regard to salary, pursue it through supervisory, union representative, or Personnel Office channels. Utilize the established grievance procedures and system and be armed with facts to justify upward adjustment of your salary.

Curb your emotions and do not make your co-worker the target of your envy or resentment. He or she is probably within the right pay range and has probably earned that status. Salary comparison has its risks, since we often do not have all the facts at hand. Miscommunication and distortion often result from a chance discussion about salaries, even from a single offhand remark. While there is no intended censorship, the prudent employee tends to avoid discussing salary for the very reason that misunderstanding can sour the relationship between him and the co-worker.

Personal Finance

The subject of money somehow triggers meekness or bravado, sometimes pretense. In any case it introduces into the budding friendship an unwanted competitiveness of the haves and have-nots. Neither brag about your assets nor probe into those of your work friend. Confine your money talk to the neutral areas—credit cards, beating inflation, home heating bills, store sales. Add to these the knowns such as fringe benefits, company-wide salary increase, interest rates, fees for child care, and other topics.

As to more personal matters—indebtedness, family status or inheritance, insurance beneficiaries, settlement of an estate, or the preparation of a will—discussion becomes appropriate only later as the friendship matures. If you both have money invested in stocks and bonds, refrain from offering buy/sell/hold tips or any other advice concerning the market. If your recommendation proves to be a dud, it will surely put a dent in the friendship, especially if there is a substantial loss.

Anticipate that your co-worker may someday need to borrow twenty until payday. Keep the amount small, and expect repayment on time. The reverse should apply if *you* should be in a pinch. If borrowing money becomes a chronic habit, find ways to turn down your friend's requests. Do not be lured into being a co-signer or endorser to a loan application. You may regret having made the commitment if the deal should later result in delinquent payments or default. Let your friend turn to the company credit union, her family, or other source for this kind of transaction. As to requests for donations, contributions, raffle tickets, or other fund-raising activity in which your partner is soliciting for an organization, use your judgment but don't be too soft a touch, nor do it too often. Join others in a pool for a winning lottery ticket (if legal) only when you feel like it. Finally, recognize that there is no need to flaunt financial independence or to feign being hard up. Most of your co-workers don't really care about your financial status—they are interested in themselves. It is only a matter of chance that you are both on the same payroll. In dealing with your work friend on all matters concerned with personal finance, be discreet and recognize the degree of vulnerability that may be involved.

Marital Relations

Your work friend will divulge only what he or she wishes to in regard to a marriage or other living arrangement. Don't be inquisitive about such matters as a previous marriage, separation, adoption of a child, concern about possible infertility, or present incompatibility with a spouse. These are intimate aspects of your friend's life, and he or she is entitled to keep them so. Only if you are a close confidant(e) should you begin to discuss these matters. Restrain your curiosity; quit citing recent columns of Ann Landers as a come-on; redirect your talk to less intimate subjects. If you push it, your friendship may be a brief one. Leave it to your friend to determine the right time and the right place to share these personal subjects, even if you are eager for the friendship to deepen.

Gift-Giving

Gift-giving between work-friends should be modest. Avoid being indulgent and suggest that your friend do the same. Limit gift-giving to principal events such as a birthday and Christmas or Chanukah celebration. An appropriate card will do for other occasions. Events such as graduation, confirmation, birth of a child, anniversaries, etc., should be kept within the family. As a friend you may send a card or flowers or make a phone call, but there is no need to send a gift.

Do not obligate your work friend by means of an invitation to a family affair; spare her the task of turning it down. There are always exceptions, of course, and your good judgment should prevail. If socialization has indeed escalated to affection, then you will have to exercise discretion as to how much more gift-giving and on what occasions. For the present, however, keep it at the level of sociability.

Children

As more of the workplace is populated by working mothers, more and more discussion of children takes place. We discuss their progress, problems, and personal interests. A discussion about a good camp, school, or college is generally one of good will and helpfulness. Think twice, however, before suggesting that his or her child join yours. You may be committing yourself or your spouse to obligations that will be difficult to fulfill. You may also subject your child to unwanted social obligations.

Discussions about children, particularly children in their teens, sometimes lead into a request for your support in their behalf. You may be asked for a recommendation for admission to a college or for a job, a credit card, or a driver's license. If you know enough about the person, you will generally give the recommendation and feel good about doing it. What if you do not really know the youngster or feel uncertain about putting your name to such a recommendation? You may have to be quite candid and tell your friend that she would do better to seek out the recommendation of one who can speak more strongly in the youngster's behalf. There is always the possibility that he may not be as qualified or as reliable as you think, and if it backfires both you and your work friend will have some uneasy moments trying to save face. Again, there are limits to pleasant sociability. Sustaining the sociability does not imply always having to say "yes" to your work friend's request.

Accepting Hospitality

This could be a sensitive area. Should you accept an invitation to visit your friend's home alone, or is it more prudent to wait until several other people are invited? However straightforward the visit may be, it can generate awkward questions and even more awkward responses. The newshounds and gossips in the office leave no stone unturned. Bear in mind that visiting your work friend's home brings you into a private domain and adds a new and more intimate element to your friendship. What you see and hear, who you meet, and how you feel about it are not for public discussion in the workplace.

A person's photographs, pets, book collection, paintings, and furniture all reveal something of the personal life of the owner. They reflect his or her taste, style, cultural bent. It may be pedestrian or pretentious. The mid-Victorian furniture may leave you cold, or a photo of Pope John XXIII may warm your heart. Children in the home also register in your mind. What if they are sloppily dressed, or full of laughter and bubbling with questions about dad's behavior in the office? Are you sure you're weighing your words carefully when you respond? You had better be!

You may observe household hygiene that is appalling—bathroom, kitchen, living room and porch all in need of a vacuum cleaner and a deodorant spray. Or perhaps everything is neat, tidy, and sanitary. Do you draw conclusions about your friend from the condition of his home? If so, would they have any bearing on the continued friendship? A garden can also reveal something about its keeper, perhaps more than we realize. The presence of a physically handicapped relative living there may arouse your concern about family loyalty or economic burden. Can you suppress your curiosity about the illness, your assessment of the situation?

A good guest sees much but says little. He lets the subjects of conversation unfold naturally and, whether light-hearted or serious, joins in with propriety. He does not violate the privacy of a friend's home by talking about it to others. Be guided by your host or hostess and what they wish to show and tell. Anything beyond that becomes nosiness on your part.

What if your friend willingly opens discussion about his two English setters, the neighbor's lawn, his cheerleader daughter, the neglected fireplace, or his collection of Hemingway's books? That is another matter. At his discretion he is free to reveal any part of his home life, and such a peer is all the more likeable because of it. You have probably encountered such people in your own workplace.

Socializing in each other's homes can be part of the work friendship, particularly as a friendship grows. Do it with propriety, both within the home and after you have departed from it.

Vacations

Steer clear of making plans for your family and your office friend's to vacation together for an extended period. In most cases even the best plan for a shared vacation involves an uneasy compromise on which both of you must bend in order to be accommodating. People differ in regard to exposure to the sun, sleeping habits, dance music, tipping for services, rusticity, and long hours of car driving. Some swim and sail, others are averse to either of these sports. Allergies triggered by country animals or overgrown grass can ruin the vacation of one but have no impact on the other. Spouses may have their own serious doubts but agree to the joint vacation plan just in the hope that it may be fun after all. The children may not get along well. Relationships become strained when the vacation turns out to be far less than desired for one reason or other. This is not to suggest that joint vacations are doomed to incompatibility or dissatisfaction, but it is probably better to vacation separately, come back refreshed, and talk about it enthusiastically.

Religion

Friends have been known to go to worship services together. Be sensitive to the inherent problems. Your coworker may be negative about religious observance and have been for many years. Perhaps he is accustomed to prayer and meditation on his own, or maybe he has no religious affiliation. His convictions are no less than those who prefer the formal place of worship. Don't push the matter; spare him or her the discomfort. If there should be a spontaneous interest in going to services together for a special Easter mass, the Yom Kippur service, Christmas morning, or other special religious occasion, this is fine. Otherwise, realize that prayer is not a part of socialization despite the image conveyed in these days of electronic evangelism.

In the event of bereavement in your friend's family, do what is proper. A telephone call is usually not expected and is regarded as somewhat intrusive. A visit by a work friend is not expected either, unless prescribed by custom such as attending a wake or visiting the bereaved family during the *shiva* observance in Judaism. A hand written note or a sympathy card is the acceptable thing.

Parting

Be ready to face up to the fact that even the most satisfying socialization may have to come to a point of decline when your work friend is promoted or transferred to another position within the company or leaves to take a different job altogether. You will have to let go, in the interest of preserving the friendship spirit. Recognize that his or her new job brings a new set of responsibilities and a new network of professional contacts. You may or may not continue to see each other outside the workplace.

Sexuality

The office romance is ever enticing, especially among work friends who relate well. Is sexuality a factor in socializing within the workplace? Yes. The difficulty of sexuality in the office friendship is a recurring topic in the media. The conclusions reached are direct and important. Most of them counsel against this kind of relationship. The reasons:

- Men and women involved are perceived in emotional and erotic terms by their co-workers and supervisors.
- Women are placed at a disadvantage from the outset; it is their careers, rather than those of the men, that are most often harmed.
- The affair between the two office friends becomes communal property in the workplace as co-workers and supervisors shift from observers to critics of social behavior. They assume the role of judging moral conduct, and subsequently can socially isolate either or both parties to the affair. An astute observer of the office culture and consultant to management expressed this view:

> "Sex in the office becomes a political issue when two people, regardless of their marital status, have an affair. It will almost always affect their

careers, despite their persistent efforts to maintain discretion and secrecy. . . .

[Even] that they are both single is immaterial. The facts are not nearly as important as what members of the upper echelon in the firm think."*

*Kennedy, Marilyn Moats, *Office Politics*. Follett Publishing Co., 1981, p. 164.

If one expects to have it all—a secure job, a lasting friendship, and a romantic or sexual relationship with a work friend—one faces almost certain disillusionment.

THE REAL AND PRACTICAL PROBLEMS OF SEX IN THE OFFICE

Practical questions arise to beset the employee and the company: Where is the line between flirtation and misconduct? And, where is the line between harassment and voluntary involvement? The answers probably lie more in peer perception, pressure, and informal controls than in individual accusation or management policy. Other than the traditional courtship in which two single employees contemplate marriage, authors of a recent study point to several kinds of vulnerable involvement:

- Sexual harassment—unwanted or uninvited sexual attention;
- Sexual relationship without marriage and where the

two parties live together openly in the same quarters;

- The illicit affair—that which involves at least one married person.

Sexual harassment, as defined by EEOC regulations, is unlawful and the initiator and/or the company are subject to penalty for being party to the misconduct or coercion. Companies have taken different approaches to curb the openly proclaimed living arrangement. They include: warning to discontinue the relationship; denial of promotion; transfer; discharge; and, the quiet pressure for resignation. Companies show general acceptance of the traditional romance and courtship of employees aimed at marriage, but frown upon arrangements that are unsanctioned by conventional moral standards.

A company's involvement is triggered by any number of considerations. Among them are rumor-mongering and possible scandal, alleged favoritism, lower morale, impairment of work performance, public image, and offensiveness to the sensibilities of other co-workers. Whether it is simply a romance or a more complicated relationship between the employees, a company finds it difficult to maintain a strictly hands-off policy. Most companies still contend that propriety, mature behavior, and sensitivity in the business place are values that must be recognized and observed by their employees.

READING THE SEXUAL CUES

For some people husband- or wife-hunting in the work arena is a reason for being there. Potential romance encourages the desire to meet a partner who may later become a mate in marriage. Today's two-gender work environment makes this more probable than before. It is good to be alert, then, to cues which suggest that a work friendship may be bordering on romance and a more emotionally charged relationship. Despite one's wishes that co-workers or supervisor would just mind their own business, the fact is that they are almost always on the scene and ever observant. Even when they do not intend intrusion or mischief, their physical presence makes them witness to the budding romance.

Among the cues to the work friendship now beginning to border on romance are these:

- The two staying after hours to work together more frequently;
- Excessive use of the telephone in hushed conversation;
- The after-work rendezvous;
- Either one delivering memos in person rather than using the internal mail/messenger service—and lingering awhile;
- Appearing together at the same meetings, when one or the other had not done so in the past;
- Talking animatedly but privately at the coffee break, lunch, or other interval;
- Exercising favoritism in work assignment, hours, or other work-related activity;
- Softer treatment in regard to work pressure, criticism or performance evaluation;
- Invitations together to quasi-business socials;
- Exchange of cards, flowers, gifts;

- The nonspeaking interlude which usually follows a spat;
- Conversation about weekend fun together;
- Quickness to rally to the defense of the partner in the event of some critical or unkindly remark;
- Good-natured teasing by the other co-workers;
- Joint vacation planning;
- Being away from the desk longer or more often;
- Knowledge of each other's personal telephone number, family incidents, birthdays, etc.

SEEING THE DANGERS

Your co-workers are, for the most part, quite neutral about the romance between the two. However, on two counts they clearly do show interest. First, if one party is supervisory to the other they are concerned about any favoritism shown him or her over the others. They expect equity in work performance evaluation and in opportunities for a pay increase, transfer, or promotion in addition to fairness in the allocation of workloads and assignments. If there is reason to suspect favored treatment they will resent the double standard. Rumors concerning the romance will inevitably spread and the nature of the relationship may be distorted. The romance becomes a vulnerable target. Second, many co-workers do not take kindly to public displays of affection and intimacy. They will expect to witness an occasional gesture of affection between two people who are in love, but tend to be somewhat intolerant and impatient if the romance becomes too obvious or has too many repercussions within the workplace.

COPING WITH DIGNITY

Make every effort to ward off unwanted or uninvited sexual attention. Your actions should be discreet but may have to be firm; some people are thick-skinned as well as overly persistent. If the harassment persists, request a private meeting with your supervisor or the company's personnel director. Both represent management and have a stake and responsibility under the law to take appropriate action. Fight for your job if you feel it may be threatened because of the harassment. If physical or verbal harassment affects your work performance or promotability, you may have to do battle to preserve your personal and economic well-being. If management stalls, plays possum, or sets up bureaucratic hurdles to correct the situation, persist in your action and pose various options for its consideration. If the unwanted suitor is a male, you can carry the battle through intervention of the EEOC or litigation as a condition of your resignation or after you have resigned. If the one doing the harassment is a female, do battle with the same determination and utilize all possible resources to preserve your reputation and your job. Keep a detailed account of every incident, action, memo, witness, threat, or record to build the case for having been subjected to unfair work conditions which deprived you of equal employment opportunity rights.

Sometimes sexual harassment can be handled adroitly. Women employees relate various ways of managing it with subtlety and with no hard feelings. Witness this tactic used by a woman approached by a male co-worker with a sexual offer. She smiled at him as she thought of the career and life she had planned for herself, and then said:

Suppose I make you a counter-offer. You are at a stage when you want to have a fling, to take a chance, to shake up your life . . . and I need to lie low and be quiet so I can work effectively. Therefore we are out of sync.

But I am willing to be your friend, and that's an offer you shouldn't refuse, because it's much easier to find someone to run off with than it is to find a friend—and a friend is worth a whole lot more in the end.*

*Shain, Merle. *When Lovers Are Friends*. J. B. Lippincott Co., 1978, p. 97.

GUIDELINES FOR THE POTENTIAL OFFICE ROMANTIC

You may, of course, find yourself dealing with a situation that is entirely different from harassment. Perhaps you invite the romantic overtures of a colleague. Maybe you even initiate them. In any event, discretion, firmness, and knowledge of the cues may not always be enough. These additional guidelines may help:

- Be businesslike rather than emotional, and think in terms of a smooth working relationship in the future.
- Do not keep telephone numbers or keys of your co-worker; if they are misplaced it will cause much embarrassment.
- If you are married, don't make overtures to someone in the office. It leads to gossip, emotional pain, and career loss to either party or to both.

- Bear in mind that sexual innuendo, veiled or open, is rude and annoying—even if no harassment is intended.
- Do not seek out your boss or your boss's boss for a romance. If anything should go the least bit wrong, you will be caught in a trap.
- Cut out the puppyish conduct with your partner in the workplace. Your co-workers understand people in love but they need not endure their antics.
- Be ready to talk straight and make the simple statement, "I'm married and I prefer to keep my marriage intact," or "I am not interested; please quit bothering me."
- When your boss persists as a suitor, ward him off with the remark, "It would be impossible to work efficiently together; it will injure your reputation and career, and also mine. That's reason enough to stop."
- If a romance or affair between two of your co-workers doesn't in any way block your own job performance or interfere with your career, keep out of it.
- Don't stoop to personal attacks, anonymous calls, or poison notes. Show maturity.
- If favoritism is evidenced and hurts your own prospects for advancement, complain but try not to let on that you know the reason (the budding romance). Reveal that information only if you should be involved in a confrontation.
- Don't harm your company. Be aware that rumor-mongering can generate scandal and this in turn can damage the company's public image. Shun the illicit affair or the continued living together with a co-worker as a topic of conversation.
- Reserve kissing in the office to express congratula-

tions, to show genuine happiness to see one another after a period of absence, or to show gratitude to one with whom you already have a warm friendship. Otherwise, it is inappropriate and a bore to others.
- Finally, do not hurt each other.

Chapter 16

Drifting Apart, Moving Forward

Friendships are not eternal. They gradually dissolve and friends drift apart. The mature adult knows that workplace relationships, like all friendships, are subject to change by circumstances of one kind or another.

A number of things can go wrong: your co-worker may be the victim of a layoff; perhaps she married and moved to another community, or left to accompany her husband because of a change in his job. Many other events could conceivably curtail your office friendship.

The most common cause for a breakup in a work friendship occurs when your co-worker is promoted to another job within the company. Often the learning process and the adjustment involved in making the transition pre-empts most of your friend's time. Higher-ranking officers now invite her to lunch and to discuss business projects in which they are mutually involved. The invitations cannot easily be turned down. There are additional meetings where her presence is required which means less time available for light conversation with her friend—possibly soon to be her "former" friend. Not only is it easier for her to make and stay friends with those on her new career level but, in many instances, the company discreetly monitors her to see how she handles the changes in status, socially and professionally. In short, there is a tendency to drift away gradually from her former co-workers despite the earlier good friendship. Of course, there are exceptions and the situation will vary as to how deep the friendship and the extent to which it is valued. It will also depend upon the moral courage of the one recently promoted. By and large, however, the scenario is very much as presented here. One must also consider that she may deliberately keep distance from others, now subordinates, in order to make some tough decisions without letting emotions or sentiment get in the way. The lesson is clear: *you have to let go*. This is one test of a good friend in facing up to the realities of the workplace.

Apart from these external circumstances, some friendships are also severed because of internal weaknesses in the friendship; it just hasn't worked out well. Perhaps promises have been broken, or one or the other fails to reciprocate the friendship as he used to. Or, he has fallen victim to the drug habit or has become an alcoholic, and your help has been to no avail. Bickering and arguing may have become frequent; these conflicts drain you physically and emotionally. Perhaps one of you has begun to indulge in far too much criticism and fault-finding. In some instances the partner no longer listens as he used to and shows little feeling in regard to your problems and difficulties. It's no longer fun to go out together socially. You are irritated by personal traits you tolerated before, or, as has happened in many a workplace, competitiveness has been injected into the friendship. The competition intensifies the stress. The ease and fun that once characterized the friendship are gone. In essence, the element of mutual trust has been eroded. A cynical observer, one who regards the notion of office friendships as ill-advised in the first place, could say "I told you so."

WHEN YOU SEE IT COMING

In most cases the break in a friendship does not come as a shock. You probably have been aware for a while that things are not quite right. Here and there an incident, a harsh word, an unwarranted criticism, a hurried visit, or an inconsiderate act is noted. You will then recall a series of other unpleasant events. The awareness comes soon that there is a crack in the wall of friendship.

Now you take stock of these incidents, and several things emerge. There's a changed attitude on the part of the co-worker; he is indifferent about whether you converse or have lunch together frequently, occasionally, or seldom. Alibis and diversions become part of the game. He forgets your birthday, breaks an appointment, fails to return a phone call, or lets you go uninformed about an important piece of news in the workplace. Impatience is also reflected in the changed attitude. A brief visit replaces what used to be a pleasant, lingering chat. At the social drink in the bar he motions the waiter for the bill before a second round. Even at the workplace he will cut short the interruption with the comment that he has a backlog of work on the desk and has to get to it. If promotion to a higher level was the cause, then you will probably detect an aloofness not shown before. While you may not take each one of these signals seriously, they eventually build a barrier, a wall. The friendship has cooled.

Another phase follows. When you finally understand what has happened, a feeling of hurt sets in, and usually with it a sense of loss. The experience brings unhappiness while the hurt persists. Afterward, some kind of introspection or self-analysis ensues and you begin to raise questions: Have I let him down or betrayed him in any way? Did I mishandle any important matter? What's wrong with me that I am unable to hold a friendship? The questions will then shift to the partner: Is it *his* fault that we're drifting apart? Has he tired of the friendship? Why? Is it really that he cannot find the time for me, or that he just doesn't care? Seeing the picture more clearly you may come to the realization that it is neither his fault nor yours entirely that the friendship has eroded. It was simply nearing a terminal point for reasons so intangible that you cannot put your finger on any specific cause. To borrow the phrase from many a broken marriage, we became incompatible.

HANDLING THE SEPARATION

One point that needs to be stressed is that you avoid the laying of blame. Blame is a way of countering criticism when one cannot take it constructively. This is a kind of ping-pong shot. It is also a device to avoid self-examination. You don't want to see a weakness in yourself exposed and so you divert it by projecting the poor image onto the other person. In essence, blame-seeking is a form of defensiveness. As a mature person, you take on a friendship as an adult responsibility. You should not breach this responsibility by indulging in the juvenile game of it's-you-not-me. Blame pulls people apart, even more than does the original reason for the rift.

Nothing is accomplished by brooding about the break-up. To brood is only to introduce more negativism. More-over, your mood is likely to show in your work perfor-mance and among your other co-workers. Put the broken friendship behind you. At the same time, constrain your-self against any inclination to speak ill of the recent friend-ship or to bad-mouth your co-worker and former friends. The workplace is not a locale from which one can with-draw. As an employee you are expected to perform up to expected standards, maintain harmonious relations with others, and observe the rules and practices. Since you are under supervision, you cannot and should not risk violat-ing any of these requirements. Self-discipline will stand you in good stead, professionally and emotionally, so gear yourself to it. After all, the friendship breakup was not a disaster but just one of those deep disappointments in life.

Expend your energy in positive directions. Work hard, keep busy, and derive satisfaction from the results. Inten-sive work is often good therapy for people trying to over-come unhappiness. Seek out new contacts and possibly new friends, either within the workplace or outside. Re-sume a former hobby, catch up on someone out of town and enjoy the reunion. Even the long ride by car or train will help clear your mind and refresh your outlook on life.

A POSITIVE OUTLOOK

Sometimes we learn from seeing things in perspective. For the period in which the friendship endured there was a positive side. You enjoyed yourself, you liked working alongside your friend. You gained new knowledge, new experiences, and new interests. In addition, you probably gained better perspective and understanding about the workplace and the work life. Some of this might even have advanced your growth and career to some extent because of the exposure and informal learning. Above all, in being able to share personal problems with your friend you were able to find relief from stress and anxiety. Try to terminate the friendship in a positive way as well. You can still be cordial even if you are no longer close friends. As you see or meet each other in the workplace, try to be friendly and pleasant. Bury the bitterness. You can still keep up with your ex-friend's interests and progress, although there is no longer a mutually dependent relationship.

A good way to retain the positive approach is to avoid any indiscretion if and when you talk about your friend. Guard against divulging any confidential or private information about his personal life. He shared this with you in good faith; do not violate that trust. You would expect the same ethical conduct of him in regard to your personal life. There should be no bad-mouthing, no gossip.

Other colleagues in the workplace have probably observed by now that the very close twosome at work is no longer the same. They probably surmise that the companionship outside the office has also diminished or ceased. That is enough to know. You owe them no explanation. However, step hard on any dirty gossip which could lead to mischief and hurt your co-worker's reputation or your own.

Finally, terminate the friendship in a dignified way.

Stand tall, and let him or her stand tall as well in the eyes of others. It is in the best interests of your own morale and the morale of the workplace.

MOVING FORWARD

The dynamics of peer-relating and friend-making in the workplace requires competence. It takes skill to build and maintain these relationships. Now you know what they are and how they are formed and nurtured. You know how to share and how to compete, how to cope with problems and how to deal with loss. You are able to think and act constructively in developing good peer relationships.

As you think constructively, so can you act productively. React in a balanced way to first impressions about work partners. Avoid being taken in, but don't be turned off too easily, either. Let a little more time and experience confirm your initial impressions. Even if you detect certain characteristics which are not entirely to your liking, give the person a chance to prove himself or herself. People can and do adapt. Your work partner may adapt surprisingly well to the workplace and to you as a colleague.

Try to see potential even in the co-worker who has been around for some time with somehow no more than a neutral feeling existing between you. Perhaps it is time to find some common ground.

A healthy frame of mind will enable you to master the dualism of cooperation and competition in your relationship. You will find yourself able to give and take criticism more constructively, collaborate better, and measure up effectively to the healthy rivalry. These are evolving skills which are always being shaped and improved. Only you can do it; it is a self-development effort. Keep fashioning it, for during your work lifetime you will always be faced with this dualism.

Face up to the fact that it is futile to expect or seek the "no faults" co-worker or work friend. He or she does not exist. We all have our imperfections. Tolerance is part of the investment you make as a good peer.

THE ISOLATION TRAP—DON'T FALL INTO IT

Now and then break away from your desk and immediate project. Visit around professionally and show interest in what your peer is working on or how he is progressing, and offer a word of encouragement or some assistance if he needs it and wants it. The isolation trap is an easy one to fall into; do not become one of its victims. Through the informal "dropping by just to chat" you give a cue to the desire for a more genuine and sustained work relationship.

A happy productive worker is one who integrates his life at home and in the workplace. While the office lights can be turned off at 5 p.m., your ideas and concern cannot. You have a stake in the company and the company has a stake in you. Your future is tied to the company's future. The professional well-being of one is akin to the economic well-being of the other. Careers are often built on this connection. The new contract, the special project with its deadline, the company plan to install a new correspondence control system, the grievance scheduled for tomorrow. These do not vanish at 5 p.m. They will spill over and continue to draw upon your intellect and emotions. Similarly, your new car, the mortgage on the house, your son's Little League game, the quarrel with your wife—these do not vanish when you leave home in the morning. Such is the impact of the work life upon one's personal life, and vice versa. Integration of the two is inevitable and desirable.

This does not mean that you should become a "workaholic." See to it that work and the company do not dominate your life. Be your own person and seek your own values and gratifications. Nevertheless, remember that much of your ego fulfillment is associated with recognition and reward earned through good performance in the workplace. A considerable part of this performance is influenced by the quality of your peer relationships as you collaborate on work projects. The results of good skills, high performance, and rewarding friendships at work will carry over into your personal life. This is part of the dynamics of your work life.

Given the odds, out of twenty-five co-workers in your midst you may perhaps form a lasting personal friendship with one or two. Perhaps these odds are not much different from the possibility of establishing a personal friendship among one's neighbors, social acquaintances, or church members. One or two real friendships, well-chosen and well-cultivated, will help make your working hours the happiest time of your day.

Several key messages are conveyed in this book: Make the most of your friendship opportunities; do for yourself and also do for others who work with you; know how to weather the storms; and help others to derive satisfaction from mutualism in the workplace. Be confident that you can, indeed, win friends and relate effectively with your peers. In the end, it is your attitude, interpersonal skills, and sustained effort that count most.

Winning friends and influencing peers doesn't just occur; *you make it happen.*

References

Block, Joel D. *Friendship*. Collier Books, 1980.

Dawley, Harold H., Jr. *Friendship: How to Make and Keep Friends*. Prentice-Hall, 1980.

Evans, Olive. "Friendship: On the Job and After 5." *New York Times*, Aug. 1, 1983.

Feinberg, Mortimer, and Aaron Levenstein. "Sex and Romance in the Office and Plant." *Wall Street Journal*, Nov. 29, 1982.

Kagan, Julia. "Survey: Work in the 1980s and 1990s." *Working Woman*, Oct., 1983.

Kennedy, Marilyn Moats. *Office Politics*. Follett Publishing Co., 1981.

Mazzie, George. *The New Office Etiquette*. Poseidon Press, 1983.

National Commission on Working Women. "Survey." *Women's Day*, Oct. 11, 1979.

Peale, Norman Vincent. *The Power of Positive Thinking*. Prentice-Hall, 1952.

Peters, Thomas J., and Robert H. Waterman. *In Search of Excellence*. Harper & Row, 1982.

Editors of *Psychology Today*. "Friendship and Alienation in American Society." *Psychology Today*, Oct., 1979.

Rohrbach, Jay B. *Work and Love: the Crucial Balance*. Summit Books, 1980.

Shain, Merle. "Love and Work Don't Mix—Or Do They?" *Working Woman*, June, 1979.

Stewart, Nathaniel. *The Effective Woman Manager*. Ballantine Books, 1980.

Sugarman, Daniel A. "How to Handle Your Anger." *Reader's Digest*, June, 1974.

Editors of *Time*. "Essay." *Time*, Oct. 30, 1972.

Turkel, Studs. *Working in America*. Avon Press, 1972.

Viscott, David. *The Language of Feelings*. Arbor House, 1976.

Woodward, Bob and Scott Armstrong. *The Brethren*. Simon & Schuster, 1979.